CHILDREN'S GROWTH
THROUGH CREATIVE EXPERIENCE

Schools Council Art and Craft Education 8 to 13 Project

SCHOOLS COUNCIL

CHILDREN'S GROWTH THROUGH THROUGH CREATIVE EXPERIENCE

Art and Craft Education 8 to 13

VAN NOSTRAND REINHOLD COMPANY
New York - Cincinnati - Toronto - London - Melbourne

Copyright © Schools Council Publications, 1974

Library of Congress Catalog Card Number 73-14358

ISBN 0 442 29997 4

Designed by Antony Atha

This book is set in Baskerville and is printed
in Great Britain by Jolly and Barber, Rugby and
bound by the Ferndale Book Company.

Published by Van Nostrand Reinhold Company Ltd.,
25-28 Buckingham Gate, London SW1E 6LQ.
Published in the United States of America by
Van Nostrand Reinhold Company Inc., 450 West
33rd Street, New York, N.Y. 10001.

16 15 14 13 12 11 10 9 8 7 6 5 4 3 2 1

Contents

Acknowledgments

We are very grateful to the Delegacy of Goldsmiths' College for housing the project and for according us facilities and privileges as members of staff of the college.

With this we wish to express our sense of indebtedness to the Warden of the College, Sir Ross Chesterman, whose wise advice and encouragement have been so generously given.

We wish also to say how much we appreciate the help of our consultative committee as a whole, and particularly of its chairman, Mrs. Margaret Horne, and of those members of the committee who have taken up time they could ill spare, to give us detailed help.

Our thanks are due for the kind and welcoming way in which we have been received in the schools wherever we have gone. We would especially like to express our appreciation to those heads, staff and children of schools where we have worked more intensively and without whose generous co-operation our study would not have been possible.

Groups that have worked with discussion material over a period of time in regular meetings were based at:

Barking Teachers' Centre, Essex.
Barton Ramsey School, Bedfordshire.
Luton Teachers' Centre.
The Onslow School, Hatfield, Hertfordshire.
Poole Teachers' Centre.
Portsmouth Teachers' Centre.
Swindon Teachers' Centre.

Other groups that have worked with Discussion Material include:

Gravesend Teachers' Centre, Kent.
Blaby Teachers' Centre, Leicestershire.
Dursley Teachers' Centre, Gloucestershire.
Canterbury Teachers' Centre, Kent.
Ilford Teachers' Centre, Essex.
Lambeth Teachers' Centre, London.
Stroud Teachers' Centre, Gloucestershire.
Warley Teachers' Centre, Worcestershire.
Oswestry Teachers' Centre, Shropshire.
Pontesbury Teachers' Centre, Shropshire.
Hipper Teachers' Centre, Derbyshire.
Burley-in-Wharfedale Teachers' Centre, Yorkshire.

Grantham Teachers' Centre, Lincolnshire.
Bury St. Edmunds Teachers' Centre, West Suffolk.
Newquay Teachers' Centre, Cornwall.
Ferndown Teachers' Centre, Dorset.
Isle of Wight Teachers' Centre (Newport).
Birkenhead Teachers' Centre.
Banbury Teachers' Centre, Oxfordshire.
Market Deeping Teachers' Centre, Lincolnshire.

Curriculum Laboratory, Goldsmiths' College, London University.
Education Department, Goldsmiths' College, London University.
Edge Hill College of Education, Lancashire.
The Albion Junior School, West Bromwich, Birmingham.
St. Mary's College of Education, Cheltenham, Gloucestershire.
Institute of Education, London University.
Institute of Education, Leeds University.
Department of Education, Brighton Polytechnic.
Scraptoft College of Education, Leicestershire.
Institute for Comparative Study, Kingston-on-Thames, Surrey.
Teachers' Course, Offley Place, Hertfordshire.
Teachers' Course, Woolley Hall, West Riding, Yorkshire.
King Alfred's College, Winchester.
Rolle College of Education, Exmouth, Devon.
Education Department, Leicester Polytechnic.
Trent Park College of Education, Middlesex.

We are grateful to the Hertfordshire County Education Officer for the permission to reproduce the illustrations on pages 94 (bottom right), 96 (top), 98 (bottom), 101, 104, 113, 118, 119, 120 (top), 121 (bottom).

7

A note on the pattern of education in maintained schools in England and Wales (for the overseas reader)

Since the 1944 Education Act, education has been organized into a Primary stage from 5 to 11 years and a Secondary stage from 11 onwards to a given minimum leaving age (now 16 years).

The primary schools are designed to serve a relatively small local area compared with those areas served by secondary schools. In them the teacher is in general responsible for all subjects in the curriculum and teaches a class for a year, or sometimes more. In some schools in recent years teachers have started to combine their classes and work together as a team, using each others strengths and interests.

The secondary schools are much larger than primary schools, usually drawing on a wider catchment area. In the main, they are in any particular area either comprehensive schools, catering for all ability-groups, or they are divided into grammar schools, with a selective entry, and secondary modern schools. Most teaching is by subject-specialists, and much of it is in rooms with specialist equipment.

The middle schools
Since the early 1960's, some local education authorities have made an alteration in this pattern by introducing a separate stage of education corresponding to the middle years of children's school life. Therefore in some areas, children of 8 transfer from the primary school to a middle school and remain there until they are 12. In other areas children transfer at 9 and stay until they are 13.
    Where these schools have been purpose-built, the buildings have reflected the educational thinking behind them. In some, there are year-bases where children work with one teacher for the basic subjects, and from which they move out into specialist areas such as those for science, for language, for home economics or for art and the crafts, where facilities are available for study in depth. Central resource areas also extend the possibilities for personally motivated work. In some middle schools, particularly those with 13 year-old pupils, there are specialist as well as general teachers.

8

The Schools Council

The Schools Council for the Curriculum and Examinations is the principal organization in the United Kingdom concerned with reform and development of curricula, teaching methods, and examination systems at both primary-school and secondary-school level. The Council, which was established in 1964, is an independent body financed by central and local government authorities; all the main educational interests in the United Kingdom are represented on it and the Council and its committees have a majority of teacher members.

The aim of the Schools Council is to keep under review the curricula, teaching methods, and examinations in schools. This is achieved through working parties, enquiries, and research, and through a range of projects on curriculum development. Many Schools Council curriculum development projects originate teaching materials based on the findings of their research and these materials are published subsequently by various firms; Art and Craft Education 8 to 13 is one such Project.

Schools Council Research and Curriculum Development Project Art and Craft Education 8 to 13

THE TERMS OF THE PROJECT

The Schools Council Research and Curriculum Development Project Art and Craft Education 8 to 13 began in September 1969 and continued for three years at Goldsmiths' College, University of London. The Project's brief entailed both research and curriculum development in art and craft education for the age group 8 to 13.

THE PROJECT TEAM

There were three part-time Directors, and two, latterly three, full-time Research Officers.

Directors

1969-70	*Charity James*	Director, Curriculum Laboratory, Goldsmiths' College. *(Chairman)*
1970-72	*Audrey Martin*	formerly Lecturer in Education, University of Leeds. *(Chairman)*
1969-71	*Seonaid Robertson*	Deputy Head, Art Teachers' Certificate Course, Goldsmiths' College.
1971-72	*Dr. Renée Marcousé*	formerly Education Officer, Victoria and Albert Museum.
1969-72	*Michael Laxton*	Senior Lecturer in Design, Department of Handicraft, Goldsmiths' College.

Research Officers

1969-72	*Helen Gray*	Senior Lecturer in Primary Education, King Alfred's College, Winchester.
1969-72	*Keith Gentle*	formerly Head of Art and Craft Department, Humphrey Perkins High School, Barrow-on-Soar, Leicestershire.
1971-72	*Ron George*	formerly Head of the Department of Art and Design, Stopsley High School, Luton, Bedfordshire.

AIMS

The initial aims of the Project were:
- to make known and co-ordinate advances in art and craft teaching, particularly bridging the gap between primary and secondary schools.
- to re-examine the contribution which art and the crafts as autonomous studies can make to children's development, and also to see the contribution they make to the flexible curricula being developed in many junior, middle and secondary schools.
- to undertake pilot experiments in the in-service education of teachers.

The team decided that its main objectives should be (a) to discover and identify, through careful observation, the nature of children's creative and inventive experience with materials, and from this study (b) to reach a finer understanding of the conditions which encourage their creative and imaginative growth.

METHODS OF WORK

The Research Officers have concentrated on studying children in various situations, rather than on 'models of curriculum'. Individuals as well as groups of children were observed in detail and extensive use was made of cameras and tape recorders to record specific situations.

Two other Schools Council projects touch on the same area, but both have been concerned with secondary education. These were: *The Design and Craft Education project*, based at Keele University, and *The Arts and the Adolescent project*, based at Exeter University.

This meant regular visits to a limited number of schools, so that the Research Officers could begin to understand the particular influences which affected the children's creative work. As teachers and children became used to their presence they were able to use the cameras and tape-recorders without creating an artificial atmosphere.

The resultant slides and taped material captured unique moments in the way that children worked. They also revealed certain characteristics and recurring patterns of behaviour, which had implications in a wider context.

The material gathered was further refined by constant reference back to the teachers concerned, so that the Research Officers were prevented from making inaccurate assumptions.

These records form the basis of film-strips with taped commentary, which we hope will be used to encourage discussions and self-appraisal by those concerned with art and craft education. The team has used these sets in discussion with groups of teachers in Teachers' Centres and elsewhere, and it is hoped that this approach to curriculum development will contribute to the work already being undertaken in in-service training.

MATERIALS PRODUCED

HANDBOOK

Children's Growth through Creative Experience
Art and Craft Education 8-13

This handbook is intended not only for teachers but for all those concerned with the education of children within the age-range of 8 to 13. It includes the findings of the Research Officers' detailed observation of children and teachers in schools, and of the conditions which favour or hinder creative work.

SOURCE BOOKS

Using Natural Materials
Using Constructional Materials
Using Objects

Three supporting books which explore in depth suggestions and ideas for teachers in relation to the three sources, which are indicated in their titles.

DISCUSSION MATERIALS

These twelve sets of discussion material are in the form of half-frame film-strips with taped commentary. These are for use by groups of teachers in Teachers' Centres, in Colleges of Education, or elsewhere.

This discussion material is not intended to direct teachers or students to any pre-determined line of development in their work, but to promote debate on the values and purposes behind art and craft education (see Appendix 2 *Discussion Material*).

TITLE	AREA OF WORK	TYPE OF SCHOOL AND AGE OF CHILDREN
Metropolis	Construction	*Comprehensive school 11 to 16 years*
Imagining with clay	Clay work	*Junior and middle schools 8 to 13 years*
Personal adornment	Craft	*Comprehensive school 11 to 12 years*
Art in transfer	Study of art/craft work	*In purpose-built middle and upper school, 8 to 15 years*
From pleasure they create	Museum studies	*Junior and grammar 8 to 13 years*
Messing about or achieving control?	Painting	*Primary 9, 10 and 11 years*
Resistant materials	Craft	*Children of all ages 3 to 18*
What have we learnt? – idea of a teachers' course	Construction	*Teachers' course and primary school, 8 to 11 years*
Fairlop environmental study	'I.D.E.'	*Comprehensive school 11 to 12 years*
Fantasy	Construction	*Comprehensive school 15 to 16 years*
Waste materials	2-and 3-dimensional work	*Village college 11 to 13 years*
Whose objectives?	Painting	*Junior high school 11 to 12 years (Leics.)*

Introduction

The Educational Scene

At the outset, the area of the Project's enquiry seemed wide and complex, covering as it did the very different educational philosophies and curricula of primary, secondary and the emergent middle schools.

This complexity in present day education of course partly reflects the accelerating change in our society. To go no further back than 1945, there have been alterations, even transformations, in the social and cultural background of our lives which have profoundly affected children's development. Today their experience is very different from that of any previous generation.

Social influences may have provided the propitious climate, but the ideas were planted by educational reformers in this and earlier centuries, who gradually helped us to understand more and more of the way in which a child develops and of the way in which he learns.

The effects of these ideas appeared first in the schools for the lowest age range, and their influence has spread upwards, from the infant schools into the primary and now into the secondary schools, with the middle schools coming on to the educational scene only in the last decade.

In the best of our primary schools education is centred on the means by which children most naturally learn, and on providing for different rates of development. Their learning is on an individual basis and its starting-point is the 'experience, the curiosity and the awakening powers and interests of the children themselves'.[1]

Self-initiated activities arise from a planned environment, the aim of which is to create a workshop atmosphere. Here the children can pursue tasks with the minimum of timetable restrictions, and class or group teaching is organized by each teacher according to the current interests of the children and the resources available to the school. The strong motivation produced by curiosity and individual enquiry is often led to develop into group enquiry and inter-disciplinary study. Unhappily, at the transfer to a secon-

[1] *The Primary School*, Report of the Consultative Committee under the chairmanship of Sir Henry Hadow (H.M.S.O. 1931).

dary school still working on traditional lines, where the emphasis may be more on the subject-content than on the child learning it, this strong motivation is often allowed to peter out. A child of 11 'is faced with a ten-subject curriculum and a bell every forty minutes', and a succession of specialist teachers, each of whom he knows very little in the first term or two. The child here moves into a subject-orientated world, where there may be no links between the different areas of learning, and the organization may allow for little flexibility. Some children find that little account is taken of their previous learning, and the size and complexity of the school tend to leave them lost and confused.

There is a resultant concern among educationists that the middle years of schooling should be part of a continuum of education, with no abrupt break at either end of these years. Hence the search for methods of transfer from one type of school to another which will obviate such a break. Partly with this end in view, the new middle schools and the secondary schools which are taking the problem of transfer seriously are thinking out the curriculum afresh for children in these years.

The creation of a new stage of education, in the form of the middle schools, has made new thinking possible, without the restrictions of traditional expectations. The setting-up of these schools has led to a revaluation of the aims and methods appropriate to this age-group. The methods which are evolving incorporate the 'best' of primary school approaches and at the same time relate the children's work to the later stages of their schooling.

It is important that these middle years are recognized as having their own validity, their own qualities. A boy or girl in these years is a person, not merely someone in the process of transition from child to adolescent. It may be that the middle years are especially important in helping him to find himself. As has been said, 'the kind of person he becomes as an adult is related in no small way to the ideas, attitudes, values and skills he develops in these years.'[1]

Clearly the curriculum for these children, if it is to 'work', must be related to the stage of development they have reached. Yet nothing stood out more clearly from our study than the marked disparity of development – physical, mental, emotional – of children in our age group, and especially in the later years of it.

Some children of 11, for example, seem to be still in the relatively calm period of later childhood; others have moved into adolescence. Many look outward, are interested in exploring the external world and in finding out how things work; but many

[1]*Education in the Middle Years*, Schools Council Working Paper 42, p. 10, E. H. Badcock et al. (Evans/Methuen Educational 1972).

seem also to need frequently to return to the inner self, and to express feelings (of which they are themselves hardly aware) in the secret language of fantasy.

Many are developing particular interests in which they can become highly knowledgeable, and are eager to become skilful in pursuit of them. In most, but not in all, there is a readiness for close co-operation with others which leads naturally into group work, and with this comes an increasing desire for the approval of their peers. Overall there is a strong tendency to seek independence of the adult, which goes side by side with wanting to be grown-up, and to enter the adult world.

In the schools most aware of the needs of children in the middle years we found that the curriculum was shaped to give opportunity for individual learning, or learning in small groups, with the emphasis on *understanding* rather than on mere memorizing of facts. This emphasis has a natural outcome in enquiry-based work, much of which cuts across the boundaries of formal subject teaching.

In this context, education through art and the crafts takes its natural place, not as an ancillary but as a mode of learning and understanding. It is no longer out on the periphery of education, but has moved near to the centre.

The team does not claim that the evidence of its work in the following chapters, and in the visual discussion material, is complete in that it covers every side of education through art and the crafts in the middle years. We hope, however, that it will help teachers to question the philosophical basis of what they do, and with increased insight to see experience in the creative arts as an essential means whereby children can grow in imagination and sensitivity.

Chapter 1

The Place of Art and Craft in Education

If one observes the activities of children in the age group 8 to 13, or indeed of any age, one is soon forced to recognize in them something of the same energy and enterprise that has impelled man since civilisation began – the impulse to explore and examine the environment by way of the materials it contains – together with the natural ability to give concrete expression to ideas, images, values and aspirations through the physical materials of that world. To deny children during their formative years full opportunity to engage in activities so deeply rooted in their nature, would be to restrict their growth towards maturity. To deny society the benefits of realizing its own imagination and inventiveness through the medium of materials, would be to stultify society itself – for that creative energy is surely one of the most significant human attributes, on which much of civilisation is built. It is therefore essential that any definition of the purpose of art and craft in education, must recognize and give scope to this human impulse.

While it is possible to identify values and purposes of art and craft education that remain constant and always relevant, others cannot be seen in such definitive terms. For in man's attempt to identify ideas and express his feelings through materials, he is affected by the constant shift in the condition and aspiration of his society. In turn, what he expresses will in some measure affect that society or environment. The Arts (including the visual arts and the crafts) are therefore as much agents of change as they are themselves determined by change and new potential in society.

Anyone who attempts to define the value and role of art and craft in education must, therefore, be as sensitive and alert to contemporary issues as he is to the fundamental relationship between man's creative genius and the materials of his environment.

WITHIN A CONCEPT OF EDUCATION

In the period in which we find ourselves, when scientific and technological advances are breathtaking both in the wonders they open up and the pace of change they enforce, attention has been increasingly given to the sciences in education. The newer methods of science teaching kindle children's curiosity and start

17

them off on the paths of enquiry and discovery in a way that can contribute immensely to their intellectual alertness and to their whole attitude to learning.

But Viktor Lowenfeld's reflection on education, made more than twenty years ago, has contemporary relevance. 'For the development of a healthy personality, it is of the utmost significance that a balance be kept between emotional growth and intellectual growth. The present system suffers greatly from an over-emphasis on intellectual growth.'[1]

The current emphasis on the intellect and cognitive development, today so seldom questioned, implies an under-valuation of the intuitive, emotional and spiritual aspects of man's nature. It tends to aggravate the deficiences already present in our culture, so adding to the difficulties and emotional problems of young people growing up in it.

Matthew Arnold defined education as 'helping a child to know himself and the world'. If one accepts this definition one is led to an understanding that the complete identity of any child goes beyond his intellect, and that in the personal development of each child education must recognize a responsibility for his total being – body, mind, emotions and spirit. Secondly, as Arnold implies, all individuals have an individual role and special responsibility, both within their immediate social group and to the community at large. Education as we see it, therefore, is concerned not only with the personal growth of each child and in developing his total identity, but also with helping him to become a sensitive and responsive member of his group and community.

Art and craft is significant in both of these aspects, for it deals with the forming and expression of ideas, thoughts and feelings through the reality of materials, and in so doing creates a bridge between the individual and the world around him. Thus opportunity to handle and explore the materials of our environment can not only encourage the individual identity of each child to mature : it can help him to relate to and become sensitive towards his environment.

To write at length of the values and purposes of art and the crafts in education is superfluous here, as these are shown in the course of the next chapters, but there is one issue which we should perhaps explore further, that of imagery.

One of the vital capacities of growing children is to form clear images, and in the work of children between 8 and 13 a whole range of meanings and functions is being explored in their image-making. The technical and the expressive often overlap.

Images of things seen in daily life mix with those from the unconscious, some of which are archetypal images of continuing significance. The portrayal of these powerful images is gradually modified by the increasing awareness of the appearance of 'real' things. It is between the ages of 8 and 13 that the inner images often crumble before the pressures of external reality, and in consequence there is a gradual eroding of the child's personal imagery. Today, the external pressures of the contemporary world accelerate that erosion.

Linked inseparably to the making of images of personal meaning is the subtle yet momentous understanding of one's own potential. 'It was more me than anything else I ever did', said a 15 year-old about his own painting. Standing as external, visible and tangible, the personal image is a testimony to the maker. It can be an answer to nagging self-doubt, or a source of the confidence so deeply needed at this critical stage of development between childhood and adolescence.

At this time, therefore, art and craft education has an especial responsibility – to preserve the strength and confidence in each child in respect of his own imagery, and further, to develop in him the power to create this imagery with courage, sincerity and vividness.

OUR BELIEFS

During our research our understanding of the nature of children's creative and inventive experience has deepened. We have become more and more convinced:

- that children's work in art and craft comes about not through exercise of any one side of their abilities in isolation but through a fusion of intellectual, emotional and physical energies;
- that for many children verbal thinking by itself is inadequate and frustrating, since their creative and sensitive energies need to be expressed in a concrete form, through visual, tactile and spatial images;
- and that through such expression of their feelings and ideas, children grow inwardly, in personal awareness and sensitivity, and outwardly in confidence and in their capacity to communicate with others.

[1] *Creative and Mental growth*, V. Lowenfeld and W. L. Brittain (5th edition Macmillan, London, 1970).

Chapter 2

The Children

Our study has been of 8 to 13 year-olds, but we found that in order to understand these ages it was important to look at development before and after these years. We were constantly aware of the effect that previous experience has on children's approach to creative work, of the wide differences in this experience and their confidence, quite apart from immense variations in all other aspects of development. Similarly we felt a need to look beyond the 13 year-old to examine some of the effects of adolescence.

BIRTH TO 8 YEARS

The young child's learning, though apparently random, is first effected through sensory experience, and the accumulation of a fund of knowledge based on sight, smell, touch and hearing creates the foundation for other learning. His view of the world is egocentric: spurred on by an innate curiosity, he explores the materials and objects in his surroundings. These exist only as they affect him and there is no separation between thought and feeling in the child's direct response to an object and the way he understands it. The image and the object are one.

Up to the age of 6 or 7 the intuitive language of ideas, gestures, sounds, words and symbols which he has built up will be a mixture of what he knows and what he feels. The spontaneous involvement and exploration of materials and objects is linked with confidence to experiment with this intuitive language. As experience increases so does the need to refine and control his actions. This control is of two kinds: *external control* over materials, objects and movements, which is shown in levels of skill and co-ordination and leads to some measure of order from which further development takes place; and *internal control* over responses and the capacity to absorb new experience, which brings harmony and confidence. This control is achieved in young children through play. The deep concentration, involvement and pleasure which characterize this kind of learning seem to be directly related to their ability to approach new experiences with confidence. In the words of D. Winnicott 'to control what is outside one has to do

Picture by Michael, aged 4¾, of his recollection of an old castle with winding steps and a vintage police car.

Drawing by Michael at 7½, of an old manor house and a castle; a skeletal view incorporating all the elements that impressed him.

things, not simply to think or to wish, and doing takes time. Playing is doing'.[1]

Up to and often beyond the age of 7 or 8, the child is frequently only able to understand relationships in concrete terms. Plenty of opportunities for direct sensory experience through handling materials are essential if the feelings and the intellect are to grow. Another aspect of the earlier years is the striving for independence and the establishment of a personal identity. It is an egocentric stage where friendships are fluid and the child is delighted with himself and what he makes. 'Look at my drawing'. 'I can paint good'. This is very different from the growing dissatisfaction shown by many children of 8 years and upwards, where they are becoming more self-critical.

[1] *Playing and Reality* D. Winnicott (Tavistock, 1971).

21

Richard, aged 11¾, was very aware that buildings have sides, and of the difference in size between one thing and another. This drawing is built up from a mixture of ideas and information and lacks the spontaneous vision of younger children.

THIRTEEN UPWARDS

The adolescent, like the child under 8 years old, is seeking independence and control not only at a physical level, but in terms of thought and expression. If the pre-adolescent wants to make things that are 'real', the preoccupation of the adolescent is 'what is reality?' and the contrast between what the adolescent knows of reality and his feelings about it causes great conflict. This is also reflected in the swing from sociability and dependence on the group to periods of withdrawal and solitary pursuits. It is through creative work that he can often reconcile his inner conflicts, and in searching for his personal identity there is a strong need to find an idiom which is a reflection of himself. This develops out of the personal language he has acquired and uses to give his ideas and feelings form. If his sensory experiences have been nourished, his capacity for expressing feeling is apparent.

The period in children's lives between 8 and 13 which we are studying is therefore one of great change. At the beginning of this time their participation in some form of art or craft is spontaneous, imaginative and full of joy, and their motivation is strong. At the end of the period the same children will be entering adolescence, and many of them will be questioning the value and point of any art and craft.[1] A searchingly critical attitude will have supplanted their carefree enjoyment and spontaneous pleasure in creating. Certain characteristic developments take place which reflect the nature of this change and children adopt strategies to cope with the increasing confrontation of reality.[2]

SEX DISCRIMINATION

Though we have not felt it necessary to define or investigate in detail the different ways in which boys and girls work, it is clear that social expectations do influence the work children undertake. These social assumptions are often further aggravated by the curriculum structure (boys 'crafts' and girls 'crafts') or by the individual teacher who limits the range of materials that boys and

A 12 year-old girl brazing pieces of wire.

[1]The Discussion Set *Art in Transfer* deals specifically with this point.
[2]The work of the *Arts and the Adolescent* project has included some important research in this whole area and the conclusions drawn from it have considerable significance when considering the role that the Arts could play in the lives of young people.

girls can use. It is clear, however, that where schools make no such discrimination there is a considerable gain both to the individual and to the group. Where the school simply accedes to convention, the boys doing metalwork and the girls doing embroidery, there is often lack of imagination in the work produced. It is as though the children respond to the convention by making the additional assumption that they should handle the particular materials in a prescribed manner. On the other hand where both sexes work together and where the rigid material boundaries are removed, the work has an additional sense of adventure and enterprise.

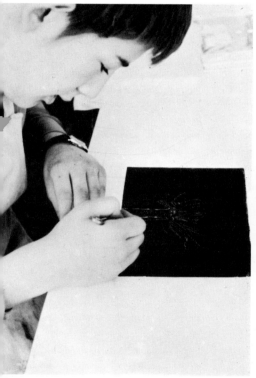

A 12 year-old boy working out a design on a sewing machine.

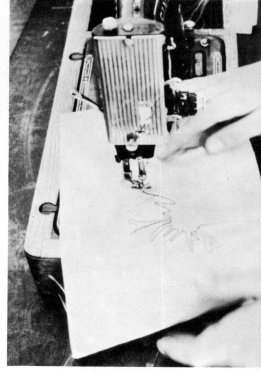

The years 8 to 13 are a stage often referred to as the 'latency period' because the strong drives, both of earlier childhood and later adolescence, are dormant, Children of this age have achieved a degree of physical and emotional independence. They are growing fast and have a capacity for absorbing information in a devoted and enthusiastic way. However, in their creative work the spontaneous confidence shown in the earlier years is beginning to diminish as they become more informed about their surroundings and as they begin to enquire how things come together and work. The random collection of 'facts' become less manageable as they

Patrick, aged 8, became interested in the camera and quickly made his own to play with.

try to translate them into images, and they see the immediate solution as one of making things 'more real' in their shape, detail and working construction (see p. 34, pl. 2). *They can no longer describe what they see in a simple way because they know too many things about it.*

The children's highly imaginative play also changes as rules

Above and below. Two 10 year-olds were illustrating a story; each drew what they felt to be important and produced widely different interpretations.

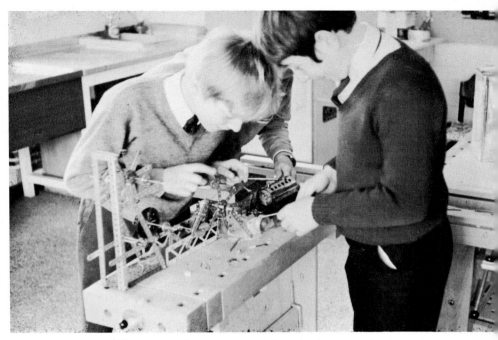

These two 12 year-old boys were using meccano to make a simple gear mechanism.

These three boys were inseparable in all aspects of school work.

27

and realism become of paramount importance. The self-absorption of earlier years is gradually replaced by developing sociability and dependence on friends of the same age and interests.

Working and Communication in a Group

There are considerable changes apparent in children between 8 and 13 in relation to how they work. Apart from the differences in levels of maturity, an 8 year-old may still be content to work alongside a friend with little exchange of ideas or sharing of responsibility on a joint piece of work (see p. 34, pl. 3). By the age of 11 groups are much more likely to plan what each member of the group will be doing and by 13 true working partnerships emerge. During these stages the dependence on and recognition of skills and abilities in others can lead to a great deal of learning.

Children begin to share a common language which incorporates attitudes, values and particular interests and is independent of adults. They communicate through language and gesture – 'in' jokes and secrets often develop as improvised drama – where ideas are played with in a free-flowing non-directional way. The contact is not just on the level of interests and action but can also consist of shared feelings in the face of a common experience. The forms and images children produce when working in a group can become powerful catalysts of communication between them (see p. 34, pl. 4). One boy we observed in a 9 to 11 primary class had a facility to 'throw together' objects in clay which had no intrinsic value for him, but involved him with other children. A child who has hitherto had little standing in the group may well be looked upon in quite a different light because of his ability, not only to manipulate a material, but to create images which the other children find unusual or compelling (see p. 35 pl. 6). It is not merely being in a group that is of importance to the child, but being able to take part in the processes of working and decision making.

Children find ways of communicating through various methods of working together, whether in friendship groups, ability groups or those based on the hierarchical structure of the class as a whole. A group may feel confident in tackling tasks which would have been impossible for one child on his own.

It often appears, however, that within the group a member has a specific role to play as an expert, an unskilled labourer, an ideas

Opposite. Having watched a boxing championship on television the children rushed in the next morning to paint the contestants. When the teacher queried the fact that the paintings all looked the same, they said 'Course they do, they're Cassius Clay'.

man or an onlooker. The security of each child knowing what is expected of him can give confidence, but is likely to restrict the child's development if the role remains unchanged and he is never given the confidence to grow outside it – the perpetual odd job man for example.

Copying and Imitating, Borrowing and Adapting

Children of the same sex often work together in pairs, drawn together by similar interests, abilities or neighbourhoods, or perhaps just personal affinity. It has become clear from conversations with children that many gain confidence through copying each other, as is demonstrated in the illustrations. The teacher – particularly in an open-ended situation – is not the child's only point of reference, and is faced with the problem of using this common pattern of behaviour to help the child become more selective, encouraging observation and helping him go beyond mere imitation.

Copying and imitating seem to be connected with skills, techniques and styles, while borrowing and adapting take place in relation to ideas, which can catch on like wildfire in any group. This indicates the acceptability of certain ideas and images to children because they arise in the group and reflect group feeling. The reality of the image tends to be of little relevance, indicating that where the idea is strong enough in the imagination to unite the feelings, self-criticism, on the grounds that it doesn't correspond to observed reality, is far less.

Although this area of motivation can be made use of by the teacher, there are dangers in borrowing. Many children gain the

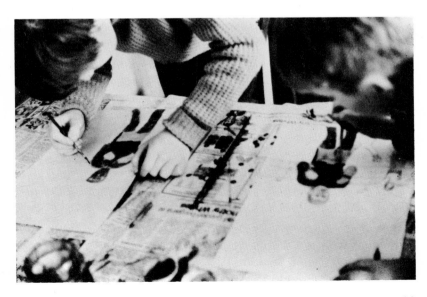

The girl on the left copied exactly everything her friend did.

These two boys worked closely together, discussing their discoveries.

confidence to adapt and innovate through first borrowing an idea and subsequently developing it further, but the danger lies when they get stuck at the copying stage.

Values and Attitudes

In groups, children take on common values and understandings independent of the adult. They will tell you who is best at art, which they may define variously as felt-tip pen drawings, cartoons (see p. 34, pl. 1), pencil copies or the more 'conventional' art as accepted by the teacher. Making things is often in another category, defined by children in such phrases as 'He's good with his hands'; 'You should see the models he's made'; 'She's always dressing dolls'. The two definitions 'good at drawing' and 'good with the hands' sum up the way that many children view success in practical work, possibly influenced by adults.

This view of art and craft is reinforced by the many kits, toys, colouring books and pastimes readily available on the market, and can have the effect of excluding many children of this age from confident participation. This is reflected in such remarks as 'I'm no good at art'. Taken to its extreme, children's preconceived notions about art and their ability to participate can be as restricting or as positive an influence as the teacher's.

The way in which the teacher interacts with these values and attitudes is crucial. If he sees the activity of art and craft only as one of creating a satisfactory end product and of stimulating a variety of contacts with different materials, the central function of any personally creative work will be overlooked. This aspect of creative work is not merely an attempt to discover and learn, it is also a medium for feeling. If the teacher has had experience of the difficulties encountered through his own creative work when attempting to find the right forms to express his feelings, he will have a deeper insight into this aspect of art and craft. As one teacher said: 'That's it really. I do feel deeply – about all kinds of things – but I haven't found a way of getting it down.' At the centre of this transitional period of development between 8 and 13 is the growing confusion between what is known of observed reality and finding a satisfying form to communicate the way in which one is affected by it. To overcome this central divergence in their creative work children adopt a number of strategies.

PERSONAL WAYS OF WORKING

Although we may identify many characteristics as being typical of this age, creative work remains a highly personal affair. This can be seen in the different ways in which children prepare for work and the value placed on the individual's response by teachers of creative subjects.

31

Preparation for Work

This preparation is a reflection of the child's personality, regardless of the way the work is initiated. Our observations of children handling different materials showed that a period of external preparation involving the organization of a work space and assembling materials and tools is important (see p. 35, pl. 5).

The approach to creative work by children under 8 tends to be spontaneous and they accept any available material in an unsophisticated way. Between the ages of 8 and 13 this approach gradually changes so that one becomes aware of new elements which might be called *external* preparation. This is closely related to previous experience; there is a 'knowingness' that increasingly replaces spontaneity and leads the individual to consider and plan ahead before the moment of contact with the material.

The very act of taking into account a number of alternatives can compromise the impulse to create. Taken to its extreme, art might be seen as only produced in the mind, and if the child actually feels compelled to produce something, he will often fall back on earlier stereotypes, which fail to satisfy him. He must be encouraged to select both what he sees, and the means he uses to put down his ideas, so that his creative urge is not stifled.

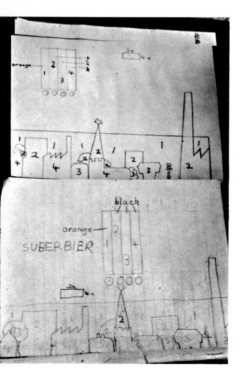

Mark devoted a great deal of time to planning before executing this low relief.

Opposite left. By experimenting Richard found out how to wire up an electric bulb in his toy car and later made diagrams of circuits for other things he had made (see p. 35, pl. 7).

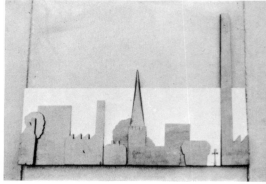

There are a variety of ways in which a child gains the confidence necessary to commit himself in a visible and tangible form which expresses his ideas and feelings. Children, like adult artists, will often use drawings and scribbles as a way of mulling over and clarifying ideas. The drawings demonstrate an increasing awareness of connections and of the relationships of space and the third dimension. Developing from this, girls read dressmaking patterns and make clothes, boys read plans and invent machines (see p. 35, pl. 7). This practical approach does not reflect the preparation which relates to feelings and emotions, but it is of central importance in the way an individual approaches the moment of starting work. Previous knowledge of a specific material and a general background of rich sensory experiences nourish the individual and contribute to a state of readiness for 'making'.

This by itself is not enough; the teacher also prepares the child, enriching his language of signs, shapes and symbols and promoting new searching and discovery. It is a similar process to the way in which the teacher builds up the child's vocabulary and fluency in speech so that he can express himself verbally. If the vital preparatory work has been superficial, the child may suffer disappointment and disillusion.

Below right. An 11 year-old used these simple scribbles in order to mull over his ideas for making a small figure.

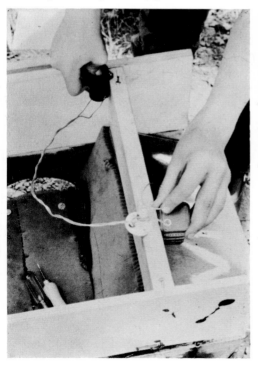
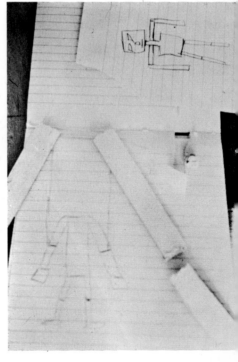

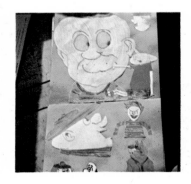

Plate 1. Top left. A group of boys in a primary class developed a great interest in cartoon drawing like this.

Plate 2. Top right. Richard, aged 10, decided to make a plan of a garden. His father said, 'Come on, I'll help you', but he replied 'I want to do it my own way, not like grown-ups do'.

Plate 3. Opposite left. These two boys worked together to make a kite and each contributed his own ideas in terms of decoration.

Plate 4. Opposite bottom. As part of a group project a class of 12 year-olds made designs in concrete with pebbles and shells.

Plate 5. Above. This little girl never started work until she had assembled all the materials she needed.

Plate 6. Below left. This boy was acknowledged to be 'good' with his hands.

Plate 7. Below right. Richard's 'Lego' house with electric light.

This is Malcolm, a 12 year-old.

Different Ways of Preparing for Work

Different personalities, both child and adult, prepare themselves for work in different ways. Malcolm, for example, a 12 year-old, is small, rather shy and retiring. He looks neat and tidy, and his work is always precise and carefully executed. He likes to assemble his tools and materials and cannot work if he is flustered. His drawing and painting reflect his way of working.

We conducted a seminar with seventeen adults to get a wider understanding of this aspect of working and, as in children, we found a highly personal approach in each to the material of his choice. One individual expressed a desire to be entirely on his own: 'I worried that I would be invaded in that little room and that I wouldn't be able to follow my ideas and feelings through'. Another preferred relative quiet but not total isolation 'I liked the seclusion of working alone, but I like people to come in, I don't like to feel that no one's going to take any notice of what I do'.

It seems that an inner tranquility or tension, evident in the focusing of the whole mind and body into a state of concentration and conscious effort, prepares the individual in a more immediate way for work.

We believe it is also necessary to consider carefully the relation-

After having had a very free experience with paint, John returned to an idiom he had already used, but was prepared to be more adventurous with the medium.

ship between a child's need to find his own way of working, and the priorities we, as teachers, feel are essential in art and craft education. It is here that the teacher can have a significant role, aiming either to focus children's efforts in the way he defines the work they do, or helping them to find personal ways of control (see Chapter 3 *The Significance of Personal Ideas*).

Personal Patterns of Work

These patterns of work vary with each person and span all variables, from the child who feels happier with a tightly imposed external pattern to the intuitive worker who adapts objectives and materials to suit his changing ideas. While one child will not be able to settle down to work until everything is in order and he can work methodically, another in the same group will approach his work in an apparently scatterbrained and disorganized fashion. The first child may be unhappy and unable to settle in a very free situation because there is too much movement and noise, and he has nowhere to withdraw to, but the latter will thrive in the same atmosphere and could contribute a great deal to the group.

If creative work were synonymous with steady progression and developing sequences of experience, then there might be a good excuse not to tolerate the personal idiosyncrasies of every child.

37

Plate 8. Top left. A fascination with bending wire gave Stewart the idea of making spectacles. He learnt how to solder and then used this in his work.

Plate 9. Left. This 8 year-old boy has made a car, and extends his play into filling it up with petrol.

Plate 10. Bottom left. The task of making a jointed figure led a boy to devote a great deal of time to inventing this solution.

Plate 11. Top right. Here the children are looking through a box of scrap televisions.

Plate 12. Bottom right. Many of the ideas which grew from this experience were later used by the teacher.

Opposite. After visiting a museum, children made their own Chinese seals of clay and soap. The teacher produced a formula for making masks from paper which the children carried out. The limited range of materials and the dominance of the teacher's ideas produced very little variation in what the children did.

Plate 13. Display of children's work resulting from this visit.

Plates 14, 15. Above. Seals of clay and soap.

Plate 16. Below. Masks.

But it is through creative work that the child explores ways of expressing feeling, thinking and imagining and, it is precisely because it is to do with his ideas, sensitivity, and perception that it cannot be standardized.

In the examples illustrated one could say that the teacher had provided facilities and materials, but it was apparent that each child achieved his own personal pattern of work and a highly individual interpretation within it. The teacher can insist on many organizational details in his room concerning the care of materials, general behaviour and so on, but he cannot and should not expect uniformity in the images the children make or how they interpret a given theme (see p. 43, pl. 21). Some children work in a way which involves routine and near-ritual patterns of behaviour, and others will be unable to start work without the constant reassurance, support and direction which the teacher can provide. This type of child may be timid and constantly concerned that what he does should be 'right' in the eyes of the teacher. He seems short of ideas or the confidence to put these into some visible form and may use the programme devised by the teacher as a secure base from which more personal ways of working may be developed at a later stage (see p. 42, pl. 18).

It seems likely that many children who feel unable to achieve satisfaction for themselves in art and craft may not have had the opportunity to discover either the material or the pace that suits them best.

The teacher's expectations or those of their peer group may also be in conflict with the highly individual strategies which children adopt in order to express themselves.

An Indian ink drawing of a small shell.

Left and below. The teacher provided the children with off-cuts of wood and wood shavings and suggested that they might like to make masks or robots.

Plate 17. Above. Simple forms of construction.
Plate 18. Below left. A dribble painting by a 10 year-old girl.

Plate 19. Below right. In order that the children could develop fully their experience of fire and kilns, a whole week was devoted to the subject.

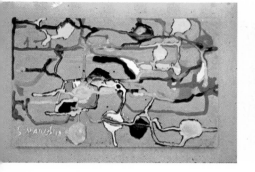

Plate 20. Above. Martin's landscape.

Plate 21. Below. The teacher provided the children with offcuts of wood and wood shavings and suggested that they might like to make masks or robots.

Although these two boys had not previously met, they got on extremely well, brought together by mutual satisfaction they derived from handling clay.

THE EFFECT OF SCHOOL ORGANIZATION

We have chosen six examples of different types of schools – primary, middle and secondary – to illustrate the kind of encouragement and opportunities children are given to develop their work patterns and express their ideas and feelings.

Primary Schools

School A was a moderate sized primary school, where there was a great deal of freedom for all children in this class of 9 to 11 year-olds. It was possible for any child to spend a lot of time in the art and craft area and art activities arose from many starting points, becoming a major form of expression for some children. The organization was free and innovative in that the teacher concerned was prepared to introduce materials and methods that were new to her and the school. There was a certain period of each week when a specific idea was presented as a means of broadening their experience of different skills and materials, but they were free to choose how they developed from this point. A high percentage of children enjoyed this form of creative work, and their approach to new materials and experience was enthusiastic and imaginative. When the class was visited by a new boy, he was immediately involved by one of the other children in using clay.

44

School B was a small, country primary school of three classes, where conditions were crowded and each child was allotted a space. Here they kept books and personal belongings. Once a week some desks were covered with paper for art and craft work. The children had been with the same teacher for two years in the top class

Above and below. A free and innovatory classroom.

Plates 22, 23, 24. Left. Dale said 'I'm not good at art'. However, when he was given the opportunity of devising ways of cutting and joining acetate sheet, he not only became technically efficient, but found he had lots of ideas he wanted to develop.

Plate 25. There are a great number of materials on the market such as 'Sticklebricks' and 'Lego' which lend themselves to all kinds of invented images.

46

Plate 26. Centre. Children study a local canal.

Plate 27. Left. Some work resulting.

Plate 29. Above. The immediate environment of the school will often be a fertile source of ideas.

Plate 28. A boy who would not accept criticism of his drawing, when given the opportunity to freely use paint, extended his work into a variety of paintings of this kind.

Plate 30. An exhibition arranged for a teachers' course.

and the three 'R's were of first importance, allowing little time for creative or inventive work. The children did not receive much in the way of first hand stimulus and worked mainly from titles. The teacher herself did not participate in creative work, but talked to the children about their work and commented as she went round the class. One child said of this, 'She never says it's all right. We always have to change things'.

The contrast between these two schools is evident in the remarks and actions of the children. The tighter and more restricting organization of School B, and the limited allowance of time and space, seriously affected the children's opportunity to work in a personal way. In School A, however, the teacher's attitude encouraged the children to find their own language, not only by providing material and time, but by her concern that the children should enrich this language through first hand experience.

Middle schools

In the next two examples an immediate similarity is apparent. In both schools the staff wanted to give the children the opportunity of a broad experience across a range of materials.

In *School C* 11 to 12 year-olds starting in an 11 to 14 middle school were taken through a number of specialist rooms, spending several weeks with each of six teachers. The work in each area was carefully arranged so that the children had a comparable experience of handling a wide range of materials. On the basis of this experience they could select three options in their second year, which enabled them to work in more depth. Time was limited to the 'rotation' between subjects. Within this framework each child had to work to a given theme from which little deviation was allowed. The specialist facilities available were good, and as the children worked in groups of 20 or less there was plenty of space. The children could produce work that satisfied them, the teacher having provided a starting point.

School D was a 9 to 13 year-old middle school with 450 children, where there was a creative studies area consisting of three rooms, for art, handicraft and home economics. In the first and second year areas there were also small practical working spaces adjoining the classrooms. The art and craft staff not only worked in their own department but were also members of teams in other parts of the school. This increased the opportunity and encouragement children had to use visual ideas and forms throughout their learning. When numbers permitted, children were also allowed to use the creative studies area to develop work from different disciplines

*These specialist areas were connected by knocking
down the intervening walls.*

Basic art forms tied to a theme.

begun in some other part of the school, for example humanities and science. Emphasis was placed on helping the children to build up a visual vocabulary, and stimulus exhibitions on topics such as line or colour were put up. The children were expected to work from starter cards and could choose to work from a variety of materials. The illustration demonstrates the fluidity of this type of organization.

In both schools there was concern to teach a 'vocabulary' through notions of 'basic' art forms tied to a theme. In School C this theme was used as a way of giving children a comparative experience of different materials, but in fact it tended to fragment their experience as they had only six weeks in each different area. The pressure on time also limited the amount of individual deviation from the theme. In School D there was greater freedom to develop away from the starter cards and the teacher's source idea, and children were often encouraged to experiment with their own ideas.

Secondary Schools

School E was a comprehensive school for 1500 children. Groups of 30 children had a double period of art per week together, whereas in the crafts boys and girls worked separately in half classes. In the first year boys did woodwork and girls needlework, in the second, boys metalwork and girls domestic crafts. In all crafts, the teachers believed that basic skills should be covered in a carefully planned way, in order to equip the children for the more complex work of the third year, leading ultimately to examinations. In art the

Working in metal and wood.

work was planned to cover specific topics within which there was freedom for personal interpretation.

In this situation there was a marked difference between the programme for crafts and that for art. In the former, a tight schedule was followed in which certain skills and prescribed processes with a pre-determined end product were aimed for. In art a basic programme of work in colour drawing, pattern and so forth was followed, though a measure of personal innovation was allowed. Older pupils were given greater freedom to develop individual expressive work.

In both examples illustrated the amount of enthusiasm was similar, but the difference in achievement and satisfaction seemed to be directly related to the degree in which each child was given the opportunity to work in a personal way.

In School E the opportunities given to the children were closely related to the syllabus, and personal ways of working were limited to the acquisition of skills rather than the development of ideas.

School F was another comprehensive school of similar size to School E. In this school, in contrast to School E, the teaching of skills was used as a means to help children develop their own ideas. There were three separate departments covering art, handicraft, and home economics. The children spent half a day per week for a term at a time in each of these areas. During one of the sessions the craft teacher wanted to introduce the children to simple forms of construction (see p. 42, pl. 17). He stimulated their interest by directing their attention to various figures made by other children,

Working in metal and wood.

Above. School E. Girls working in a workshop.

and provided a wide range of scrap and new materials which they were encouraged to use in any way they wished. As constructional problems arose, the children were helped to find a way round them.

Summary

It is obvious from these examples that the situations in which children work are 'programmed' in various ways, depending on the type of school and staff, the training and experience of the teacher and the facilities available. Within this context, the individual class or specialist teacher has a measure of freedom to create his own programme. Such programming can form a creative or conversely a limiting framework in which the child develops his personal pattern of work.

RHYTHMS OF WORK

We became aware, when working in a group alongside other people, of the different pace at which individuals move and work and that this is connected to a life rhythm which colours all thinking, feeling and doing. Similarly we have been struck by the widely differing tempos at which children work. The divisions of time in schools seldom correspond to children's individual rhythms but are generally established through precedent or expediency (see p. 42, pl. 19).

We believe that many children find it extremely difficult to fit into these unit rhythms which are the basis of school life. They become only superficially involved in what they do or develop a pattern of work that is trimmed to the timetable. Children become adept at devising ways of coming up with the answers and excluding their feelings from what they do; their personal ways of working are used as a device to protect feelings.

It seems that the lack of opportunity for children to have sufficient time to involve themselves wholly in their work reinforces the apparent separation between the feeling and intellectual aspects of their life at school, and they experience frustration and 'blockings'. At worst a child's feelings *do not* connect with what he is expected to do.[1]

Time is therefore a critical factor in enabling children to find a language through which they can bring their feelings into a state of harmony.

[1]This conflict is brought out clearly in the Discussion Set *Fantasy*.

In this primary classroom, a whole week was devoted to using paint, words or mime as a form of expression. The classroom was divided into the three areas by using cupboards as partitions. Plants were brought in as an added stimulus. The children used these in painting and in mime sequence to music. They also rearranged the furniture to make a tunnel through which to crawl and thoroughly enjoyed using make-up as another extension of their work.

In order that the children could develop fully their experience of fire and kilns, a whole week was devoted to the subject.

Clay relief done by an 11 year-old.

Chapter 3

The Significance of Personal Ideas

For most children the teacher's ideas, help and encouragement are essential starters and supporters for the development of their own creative work. The main problem facing the teacher is when to intervene. At one point children expect to be taught in order to become better informed and more skilful, and yet want to be left alone to work in their own way and at their own speed, as the following statements indicate: 'It's better when the teacher isn't there 'cos you can use your own ideas'. Andy, aged $10\frac{1}{2}$, after a session when his group in the primary school had been left on their own without the teacher. Richard, aged 12, commented on the need to experiment with expanded polystyrene for three weeks for two hours per week without the help of the teacher. 'Well, it wouldn't be our work if it wasn't our idea'. 'We work it out for ourselves, if we get stuck we ask the teacher' – three boys of 11 to 12 talking about their piece of combined craft work. Martin, aged 15, commented about a landscape he had painted: 'The painting brought out the conflict between what I wanted to do and what was expected of me' (see p. 43, pl. 20).

It is extremely difficult to talk with children on this level unless the grounds for mutual confidence have been carefully prepared, and the atmosphere created by the school and the teacher is sympathetic to the children expressing their feelings and ideas in some form. Although some children will have neither the language nor the inclination to talk about themselves in this way, our close observation of children working revealed the importance they attached to their own ideas. The situations we have illustrated seem to indicate that the children have reached an age where their ready acceptance of the help the adult had to offer (however kindly intended) has disappeared and the need for independence of thought and action is of greater importance than help.

PATTERNS OF UNDERSTANDING

We observed in children a personalized form of thinking and imagining independent of adults, which helps them in their understanding and gives them confidence to pursue new experiences.

Bruner, commenting on the work of Piaget in *The Process of*

Richard experimented with polystyrene.

Diana, aged 4, has added a pointed hat and decorative costume to her schematic figure.

Later, at 4½, she longed to be like Mummy, with long hair and pretty dresses. Notice also the eyes.

One of two clay reliefs done by 11 year-olds (see page 56). Here the schematic representation of the figure has been added to because the clay allowed the child to build up an image.

Education, wrote: 'Research on the intellectual development of the child highlights the fact that at each stage of development the child has a characteristic way of *viewing the world* and *explaining it to himself*'.[1]

Through achieving some measure of physical and emotional control, patterns of understanding develop through which further control becomes possible. Anyone who has watched children over a period of time drawing or building from scrap material, must be aware of the persistence of certain personal schemata.

[1] *Towards a Theory of Instruction*, J. S. Bruner (Harvard University Press, 1966).

Each child develops these schemata through understanding, and uses them to incorporate new knowledge and ideas.[1] Personal ideas seem to particularize experience, and to build up confidence in certain areas (see p. 38, pl. 8).

An awareness of a child's own ideas can help the teacher to understand how he learns and the possible direction in which this learning can be furthered. A child's ideas also have the power to focus his energy – and where they are not taken into account this important source of motivation can easily be dissipated.

Each individual has an internalized pattern of understanding from which personal ideas come. In a young child – under 8 years old – this pattern grows spontaneously through the senses in direct interplay with his immediate surroundings. Around the age of 8 the child becomes aware that his imaginative view of the world is different from the way things actually exist. His ideas will come from an increasingly objective experience of real things. Many children become mines of information, avidly collecting or following particular interests. They assimilate all kinds of new information in their inventive playing, talking, drawing and making. Often there is no sequence or logic about this – rather, an

[1]This aspect of children's learning and how a teacher relates to it is developed in the Discussion Sets *Metropolis* and *Imagining with clay*.

These are three different vehicles made by Richard over a period of 18 months.

apparently arbitrary and haphazard association of ideas and actions.

Increasingly the power of 'real things' and 'factual knowledge' begins to dominate the child's attitude towards his own creative ideas. He becomes dissatisfied if they do not 'work', if they are not detailed or their shape is inaccurate. He rejects the language of forms and images he has already evolved as 'babyish' and 'not right'. It is difficult for him to realize that it is precisely his personal language which both enables him to interpret objective reality and relate it to his own imaginative ideas. This is accentuated by the fact that children around him will be attempting to 'represent' the observed world in more adult ways, an approach encouraged by many adults.

Children between 8 and 13 still do have imaginative ideas which act as a strong source of motivation, and it seems that they go underground rather than drying up completely.

PERSONAL IDEAS AND MOTIVATION

We have been astonished at times by the devoted way in which children will work at some self-appointed task, with a purpose and energy which completely absorbs them. Mundane and often tedious jobs are undertaken in order to achieve a future goal, either in a group effort or an individual piece of work.

Personal motivation led one boy of 11 to sit by a river bank for hours on end while waiting for a carp to bite, a self-discipline which he found quite impossible at school.

This motivation can produce the centring of physical, intellectual and emotional energies on an apparently irrelevant object.

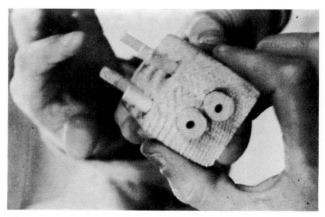

Andrew, aged 12, brought a dice to school and with his friend Stephen decided to make a 3-dimensional dice in wood. They became completely absorbed in the work, and centred their physical, intellectual and emotional energies on an apparently irrelevant object.

One could dismiss what these boys did (see illustration) on the grounds that their ideas were impractical in terms of craft, yet the ideas carry great potential for new learning. The importance of these ideas must be stressed because:

- They arise at the intersection between objective reality and the inner reality of the imagination.
- They are the means whereby feelings enter understanding.
- They enable the child to believe in what he does.
- They act as a vital focus of creative energy.

IMAGERY AND PERSONAL IDENTITY

It would be unusual to find children under 13 commenting as objectively on their work and themselves as Martin, aged 15: 'It was more me than anything else I ever did'. However, one can find such feelings of intense identification in younger children, and these feelings should be respected. The work of these children is a direct expression of the way in which they feel and the particular manner in which they see; in this sense their work is a reflection of themselves. One effect of moving from this egocentric relationship to the world is that the child loses his unquestioning view of himself, and becomes increasingly aware of himself as others see him. This affects his image-making in particular, for here there is a degree of permanence in the exposure of himself. The forms and images he creates contain his thoughts, ideas, feelings and understanding in a tangible form that exists, however briefly, for all to see, question and criticize. In spite of the fact that he may still think, dream and imagine, the child can learn all kinds of ways of hiding his feelings in what he does or makes and through these can be led to acquire a language of clichés which effectively disguises his personal imagery. Unless he finds the outer support or inner resource to go on developing his own way of doing things, he will become less able to identify who he is and what he really feels.

The search for personal identity, which becomes dominant in adolescence, now becomes a deep underlying theme. Each individual's internalized pattern of understanding is derived from many experiences, associations, events, thoughts and feelings and is 'of the essence' of himself. If a child's work does begin to express something of *what he is as a person*, it will be because his work contains more than an accumulation of knowledge and skills, borrowed and adapted ideas, mannerisms and abilities. All these form the basis from which work can start, but they must connect with his feelings in a way that invests the resultant forms with personal meaning. It is through this kind of connection that self-realization dawns and identity is found and expressed in the forms and images children produce.

Drawings of vehicles done by children of different ages.
This series of pictures demonstrates the change from a child's schematic drawing
to a more inventive approach, showing an increased knowledge and awareness
of the things around him.

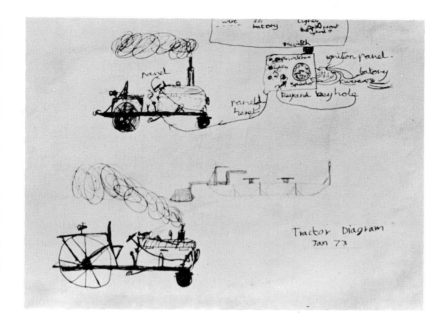

THE PARTICULAR FUNCTION OF ART AND CRAFT

One particular function of art and the crafts is to heighten visual
and tactile perceptions of the forms, colours, and textures in the
world around, but this awareness of the environment is not
limited to art and craft alone. It is an important element in many
other areas of the curriculum such as history, geography and
science, where the accurate observation and recording of information is an essential part of understanding and gaining insight into
how things have evolved. Young children see things in a general-
ized and undifferentiated way and are more concerned with associations and emotions connected with an object than with its
analysis. Specific information can be absorbed and understood
according to how their outlook is focused. The careful drawing of
a plant form may start as an attempt to understand how the parts
relate to each other, but may develop into a highly personal interpretation which adds a feeling for its beauty and form to an intellectual understanding of the form. Children experience objects
in a total way. They respond on an intellectual level, accumulating
and relating the facts that are necessary to develop this understanding, and on an emotional level, where the experience evokes
a whole range of associations, imaginative ideas and images.

Both kinds of response motivate effective learning in which visual statements play a significant and often vital part. Children's learning is invested with personal meaning through the connections made between what is seen, understood, and felt. It is as important to see the drawings, paintings and objects they make as statements of their understanding and feeling, as it is to see them as practical observations or art or craft objects. In such statements each child is evolving a language of his own through which his sensitivity both to himself and what he makes is heightened.

The specific role of art and craft is to help the child to enrich and extend this visual language which can then act as a fusion between thinking, feeling and doing. The sheer joy, pleasure and deep satisfaction when ideas materialize is unmistakable; as one teacher said: 'You can see by the light in their eyes'. As individual solutions begin to work, despite set-backs and frustrations, the child's belief in his own language is vindicated. The opportunity to use materials in a whole range of ways reinforces this belief in what he does, and makes art and the crafts significant agents in children's learning.

The same thistle drawn at the same time by 11 year-olds.

The way in which children of different ages use objects in their play. The girl of five is happy to play with a random collection of objects. Her 8 year-old brother knows more about cars (see page 38, pl. 14). He has made a car and extends his play into filling it up with petrol. Another brother of 10½ is much more concerned with making the car function and spends a lot of energy devising a brake for it.

Chapter 4

The Teachers

The ideas regarding children's creative work which are developed in Chapters 2 and 3 form the basis of our belief in the way in which a teacher should approach his work with children.

In what we have already written it is quite apparent that the years between 8 and 13 are a time of great transition in children's development. For this reason alone, the demands on a teacher vary enormously (see p. 38, pl. 9). An immature 8 year-old needs the security of a continuous relationship with his teacher, where learning is wide ranging and not limited by subject boundaries. The demands of a 13 year-old require a teacher who can help him achieve competence in serious tasks in an adult way; he will be developing more specific skills and interests, and wishing to pursue them in greater depth. Such a change in emphasis in how children learn must affect the approach of the teacher. A less easily defined change comes about through children's increasing

awareness and knowledge of real things which can overlay their imaginative experience.

It is therefore a clear responsibility of the teacher to have some knowledge of the kind of maturational development which is taking place in children throughout the age range. This is particularly necessary in regard to changes in the child's response to reality, the growing separation between knowledge and feeling, and the crisis this brings about in his confidence to express both what he feels and knows. Any effort to understand the child is closely concerned with knowing how best to help him, whether by quiet stimulation and coaxing or direct demands and insistence. This is highlighted in the following comments by teachers: 'I know art is important for them, but I just don't know how to help them when they bring work to me'. *Primary school teacher.* 'There's no value in letting them sit and fiddle aimlessly, nor in standing over them. You have to steer a middle course'. *Specialist art teacher, secondary school.*

'I can't bear to see children getting nothing out of their work with me. However much I try to help them they still want to do things their own way but don't seem to know how'. *Primary teacher working with 9 to 11 year-olds.*

The action a teacher takes will be influenced by a number of considerations apart from the age and maturity of the child. On the one hand he will feel an obligation to achieve results and standards from the children which justify his work and can be assessed by others, whether they are colleagues, the head teacher or parents. On the other hand, he will feel concern for those things which are less easy to evaluate such as children's motivation, self confidence, social awareness and imaginative ideas.

Furthermore, a teacher's training will considerably affect the way he approaches his work,[1] although this may be modified by the particular school in which he teaches. Underlying all these influences will be the personality of the teacher and the way in which he relates to children.

The confidence a teacher feels in his actions must arise through dialogue with the children, through his understanding and interpretation of the way they respond to his teaching and through the trust and enthusiasm he engenders in them. This confidence should also arise from the value the teacher places on his own work and an awareness that he can learn from the children.

THE GROWTH OF CONFIDENCE

A teacher's confidence is derived from certain satisfactions he

[1]See Appendix 1 *Art and the Education of Teachers.*

finds in his work. The explicit satisfactions are likely to be approval and recognition of what he is doing and the way in which children behave and achieve results. The implicit satisfactions are the heightened sensitivity in the children's responses, their increasing skill and confidence to express themselves and the way in which understanding can lead them forward to new discoveries. These implicit rewards are difficult to agree about and measure. They may also blossom forth into desirable results and achieve, on the way, significant advances in children's learning. Insistence on achieving these results can, however, lead to a dependence on them which will be reinforced by parents and children. Over-emphasis on the 'finished product' can limit children's image-making, narrow the range of opportunities open to them and place the teacher in the position of arbiter and judge rather than catalyst and inspirer (see p. 39, pls. 13-16).

After visiting a museum, children made their own Chinese seals of clay and soap (see p. 39, pls. 18-20). The teacher produced a formula for making masks from paper which the children carried out. The limited range of materials and the dominance of the teacher's ideas produced very little variation in what the children did.

The teacher must therefore have confidence to aim first and foremost to enrich the content and quality of children's experience; central to this task is the teacher's sensitising children to the quality of materials they use and the images and interpretations they create. His concern should be to value their capacity to think, to invent and to create with imagination and conviction at whatever level this takes place.

71

WHAT ARE THE OPPORTUNITIES?

When he first enters a school, the teacher is faced with the apparent task of teaching a large number of children as a group. Although various forms of example and advice will be available for guidance, he will have considerable autonomy in the way in which he interprets his job. Furthermore, any opportunity for children to express their ideas and images through materials will depend to a large extent on the values and attitudes he brings to his teaching.

The teacher will usually have complete responsibility for the organization and appearance of his room. If the general educational climate is sympathetic to 'individual enquiry', he may arrange his room so that a variety of activities can take place at the same time. This requires careful consideration, whether it is to introduce fabric printing into a specialist art room or clay into a primary classroom.

Many teachers face the difficulties of inadequate facilities, poor buildings, too few materials and insufficient money. Although everyone concerned with improving the quality of each child's experience should attempt to better the conditions under which children work, these things in themselves should not be advanced as reasons for giving children inadequate opportunity for creative and imaginative growth. Every group of children and each school situation presents a teacher with a different set of problems and possibilities; those of timetabling, organization of resources, locality, buildings, home background and environment, but the real answer must lie in helping teachers towards a personal conviction in the work they are doing.

Primary school classroom.

The exterior of a Victorian primary school in London. Surroundings like this do not necessarily inhibit creative work.

Primary classroom in old buildings in which the teacher manipulates furniture and space so that, in spite of the lack of room, storage space and a sink, a variety of work is going on.

In both the examples below, it is clear that the teachers have introduced a wide range of things to see and handle, and have used these to stimulate ideas in the children.

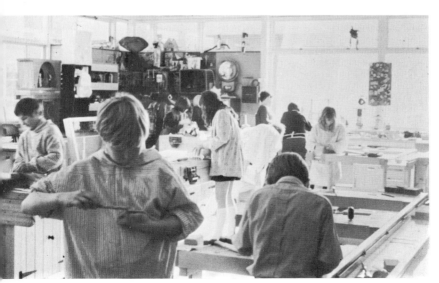

Secondary school workshop.

73

THE MAIN DILEMMA

In art the freedom for children to do things their own way has, for many years, been considered essential. There are however, many teachers who feel that 'free expression' with a minimum of teaching leads to children experiencing difficulties in handling materials and results in a loss of purpose and direction in what they do. These teachers have attempted to find ways to support and encourage children to accept greater control and rigour in their work. Our careful study of the teacher at work, in a number of different school 'types', helped us to pinpoint influences that affect the teacher's approach in this way.

In Primary School B the various aspects of school life were firmly structured. The top two classes had a detailed timetable, the teachers had separate rooms, and the children had set places in class. Much of the work was derived from television programmes and books, and the main concerns of the teachers were numeracy and literacy. The inflexible and academic approach of the teachers tended to block the creative outlets available to the children, and art and crafts had become no more than a peripheral activity.

In contrast to this the head teacher in Primary School A believed in the importance of creative experience for the children.

Free painting by 9 to 11 year-olds in a primary school. Many teachers feel that this kind of free painting is purposeless.

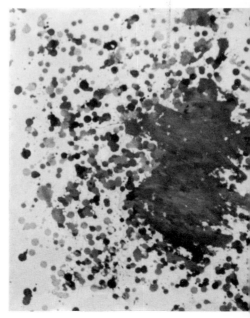

This box is typical of work produced in a teacher-directed situation. Much of the spontaneity of the children's experience with material is lost as a result of over-direction by the teacher.

Two teachers had decided to work co-operatively, linking their rooms by taking down a wall so that they could share different strengths and interests. This integration produced a greater flexibility, and the teachers were able to understand the differing needs of children, often preferring to work with small groups and individuals. The co-operation of the two teachers, with the support of the head, produced a situation where art and crafts were a far more central force in the education of the pupils than in Primary School B.

It is not easy however, to find the right equilibrium between personal expression, which may lead to indifferent and careless work, and the over-controlled approach which can stifle imagination and originality. In practice this can only be worked out with each group of children. We are sure, after observing and talking to many teachers, that an awareness of this continually changing equilibrium contributes significantly to a teacher's success.

This kind of awareness is particularly necessary in the crafts, where more resistant materials are used. The over-riding importance of skills is still stressed by some teachers, as reflected in the comment of a craft teacher we spoke to: 'There are over 200 different tools and processes these children have to know about. If all are allowed to do their own work, it encourages sloppy craftwork and lowers standards'.

Although we can understand this teacher's concern we feel that his objectives are very narrow in the context of the child's creative experience. In this teacher's secondary school the departments of handicraft, home economics and art are all kept quite separate, and the approach in general is narrow and vocational. The personal creative work of the children therefore suffers.

Many teachers have realized that a didactic approach to skills and techniques does not necessarily lead children to understand the processes involved. To a child, the lack of a necessary skill may of course mean that he is frustrated because he cannot achieve what he has in mind. However, where he is encouraged to invent and originate his own solutions, there is more purpose and meaning behind his learning of skills and techniques (see p. 38, pl. 10).

The answer to the problem 'When, if ever, do we teach skills?' is 'when we have given the child the confidence to attempt his own ideas but realize he needs to be given direct help or support in a particular way'. We believe that the objective should not be the mere achieving of competence, but helping children to find the right material and form for their ideas. It is within the context of the attitudes and approaches which a teacher builds up over a period of time that he decides how and when the teaching of skills is relevant.

We stated in Chapter 3 the importance of allowing children to develop personal ways of working. Many teachers we met encouraged this in their children, whether within a stated brief or from some less defined stimulus. In our study of Secondary School F, for example, we found that the handicraft teacher believed he was not concerned with future vocational training but with helping children to think creatively. 'I want to create an atmosphere of enquiry, discovery, and inventiveness, to which children feel confident to bring their questions, ideas and knowledge. They must be encouraged to work these out in material forms in their own way – but supported with help and advice' (see p. 38, pls. 11, 12). In a room that was alive with pictures and objects the teacher discussed with his pupils themes and projects that took shape gradually and moved naturally across subject boundaries.

The central problem for these teachers is that of finding a balance between passively holding back or actively directing. There can be no generally accepted solution to this, and there should not be one. The sensitivity of each teacher's response to his children would be invalidated if there were. It is this sensitivity which we believe teachers should have the confidence to cultivate.

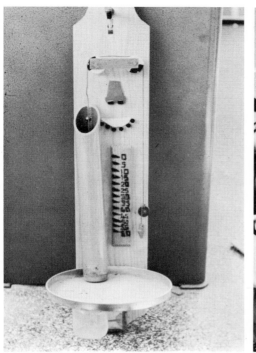

This water-clock, devised by a boy of 11, combines a scientific understanding with a personal and humorous solution.

After experience of a sawdust kiln, the children were taken a stage further by learning about glazes and by having a Raku firing.

These two boys opened up a new field of enquiry by asking the teacher 'Are medals jewellery?'.

It is in the different answers that each teacher finds with particular children that the real value of his teaching lies. For a well thought out lesson which has been carefully prepared can still result in occasions for teachers when:

- A child's responses and ideas at a particular time modify or oppose the teacher's plan.
- The child's inherent personal way of working contradicts the methods the teacher wishes him to adopt.
- The teacher's way of seeing and understanding does not recognize and allow for the child's personal interpretations.
- The teacher feels that future progress is dependent on learning a skill and the child has not the foresight to see this.

These statements suggest that the teacher must tolerate a considerable degree of uncertainty in the way he relates to the imaginative and creative aspects of children's learning. Even when he is certain about the kind of material he wants to be used, expects a particular range of results and insists on a specified approach and method, he cannot be certain about the quality of the experience nor its value in terms of the child's learning. Some teachers find this particularly stimulating. One secondary school teacher said 'For me, uncertainty is an essential aspect of being alive'. We believe that a degree of uncertainty about the outcome of creative work with children is an essential element in any approach to art and craft teaching, and should be taken into account both when planning and assessing its results. This is also necessary because the time spans needed for different individuals to assimilate and apply any given stimulus in an imaginative and personal way vary considerably. Further, it is the particular relationships, ways of seeing and responses that are significant in any creative work. It is through these experiences that individual sensitivity and understanding develop.

We therefore have to consider how a teacher can take positive steps to support and nourish imagination and feeling in children's learning, with the imparting of skill, technique and knowledge as subordinate yet essential to this fundamental aim.

Chapter 5

Towards Solutions

'The art teacher should have an understanding of a child's feelings, which motivates what he does and how he does it. Another part of his role is to help children to grope towards appropriate forms of expression for their ideas and feelings, to make images which they find satisfying. Pleasing artifacts will inevitably attract attention and be approved, but the main reason for art education does not lie in the production of artifacts but in the pupil's efforts in making them, to communicate, design, to invent or just to come to terms with life.' This is how a headmistress outlined the direction in which art and craft teachers should be moving to seek solutions.

In order to achieve this the teacher is faced with a number of difficulties, two of the most considerable being:

● The way in which a thriving, dynamic, creative environment can be built up so that children actively participate in it, where ideas can grow and children can feel free to question and experiment.
● Ways of helping the children to extend their work beyond the gimmick, the slapdash, the mediocre or the copy.

If the teacher wishes to do more than go through the motions of giving children art and craft lessons and seeks more than a selection of the 'best' work for display these two problems must be faced sincerely.

THE USE OF TEACHING SPACE

The environment of the classroom (see Chapter 6 *The Creative Climate*) mirrors the purpose and values of the teacher. From the various displays of work children learn what is expected of them and what is approved. Using the teaching space in all kinds of ways, the teacher can open up the confines of his subject and show that ideas and inventiveness gain as much respect as skill and technical knowledge. The resources which a teacher accumulates in his room can support him in operating a more flexible approach to the way children learn. This we found in Secondary School F where the teacher had a keen interest in the local environment and was alert to the potential sources of materials from industry and trade. The father of one of the pupils was employed in making car bodies and a project arose from this. This type of approach may, however, lead the teacher to work through individuals rather than a large group, and he may be faced with having to cope with many different activities, materials, rates of working and results. Changes in objectives are implicit in any departures of this kind and the direction of the children's response is away from

- uniformity towards diversity
- dependence towards independence
- acceptance towards questioning

In order to support such radical changes the teacher must organize and think about his resources in new ways and there is clear evidence that many teachers, particularly in junior schools and middle schools, are doing this.

Making a hovercraft. These illustrations show two boys working together, the plan from which they worked and various stages in the hovercraft construction.

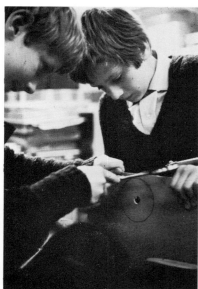

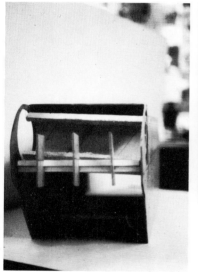

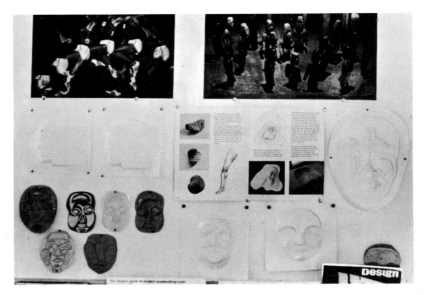

During the course of a term's work, which was inspired by a child's question about making irregular forms like cars, a whole series of work was done based on formers and the building up of complex forms such as boat hulls.

Bootmaking was an extension of this idea.

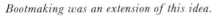

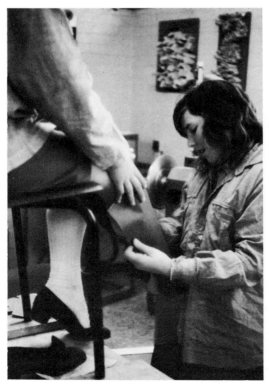

WORKING TOGETHER

It seems important to mention here the new freedom that the middle schools present in that the pressure of success in public examinations is not an immediate concern. This is seen by many

Handicraft and art teachers used paper with 11 to 12 year-old children. In the first illustration, the teacher has developed the work from a fairly tight technical exercise of rolling paper. In the second, the teacher gets the children to look at and interpret natural forms. Both gained immeasurably from discussing what they were doing.

teachers to be a release, an opportunity to collaborate with each other more and to use more flexible timetables. We found at Middle School C, where a wide range of materials was available to children and the teachers provided a broad exploratory experience across a number of different materials, that the teachers made these comments: 'You can gain a great deal from seeing how someone else tackles the same theme in different material, and this broadens your own horizons, and I've learnt a tremendous amount through being in touch with my colleagues.' We saw similar advantages at Middle School D where there was a linked all-purpose art and handicraft area, with a specialist teacher working in each, taking turns to initiate new themes. The teachers were also timetabled to share in the general work of the school curriculum. At one time a piece of 'art' work would develop in its own right, and at others art would work hand in hand with science, history and other subjects on the timetable. Children therefore had an opportunity to relate ideas back to visual and tangible forms at any point in their learning.

THE TEACHING AREA

Although it is important to provide these types of teaching spaces which can be opened into each other, it is also necessary to enable a teacher to have his own area. It can be as harmful for a teacher to feel baseless and unable to be identified with any particular place as being isolated in a box-like classroom. Nevertheless, the benefits of working in a group that has had time to grow together in sympathy and mutual trust can be immeasurable. Teachers can not only contribute their strengths but genuinely share their problems. The co-operative ventures we have already mentioned, and the many others we have seen working, have indicated that this form of organization does assist teachers in achieving greater diversity and individuality in children's learning. Further, interdisciplinary teams of teachers seem to provide a particularly relevant way of teaching children between 8 to 9 and 13 where the specialist's role is informed more by the interests of the children than by an abstract body of knowledge.

HELPING CHILDREN EXTEND THEIR WORK

Children in the 8 to 13 age group are experimental and inventive, and this method of coming to terms with real things tends to replace the fantasy play of younger children. The motivation to investigate a new discovery or experience at a deeper level is very strong and a specialist working in a team can facilitate this

This boy was given the opportunity to cut up tin cans and the teacher anticipated his need to use a soldering iron.

(see p. 46, pls. 22-24). Yet very often the specialist working on his own can unwittingly set impossibly high standards or pursue purely aesthetic interests, and therefore exclude many areas of real motivation which happen to lie outside his chosen field.

Whether the teacher is a specialist or not, he has to distinguish between providing all the answers and opening up the thinking and feeling of the child. To assume that instruction or direction will affect a child's feelings and perception is too limited a view of teaching. Children will imitate and produce work to satisfy their teachers, but this will often be rejected when they create from some deeper conviction or more honestly felt purpose. One of the teacher's main responsibilities is to recognize the import-ance of children's ideas, for when the motivation arising from these is used constructively it provides the strongest driving force in their work.

In this area of motivation children's learning can be extended not only through providing a variety of first hand experiences but by offering children the opportunity to bring their interests, questions, and ideas into the arena of their work at school. By

This boy was considered the best draughtsman in the class by the other children, but the teacher wanted to extend his use of materials and the kind of images he produced. Many children in the form were adept at producing cartoons like this. The boy would not accept criticism of his drawing, but when given the opportunity to freely use paint, extended his work into a variety of paintings (see p. 47, pl. 28).

relating these to the materials the teacher provides, their personal language of marks and images can be strengthened.

Often children will return to a stereotype, sometimes collectively; it may be a cartoon or schematic approach to drawing. The teacher, rather than disapproving of this, can lead the children forward and away from it, encouraging them to look carefully or to handle another material (see p. 47, pl. 28). In this way the confidence children feel in their stereotypes is not thoughtlessly destroyed, and an attempt to understand and share a problem can be more effective than assuming what is wrong and instructing them in a solution.

The teacher can widen children's horizons not only by encouraging them to develop their own ideas derived from sources outside the school, but by presenting them with situations and concepts they would not otherwise meet. These may be used as opportunities to evoke a whole new range of responses through which the teacher can heighten children's sensitivity and awareness. Within the field of art and crafts this could involve exploring the qualities of natural and man-made materials and considering elements such as texture, colour and the problems of space. There are many ways of doing this; the experience of looking

Children drew each other to make a group picture of themselves in the playground. The teacher was then able to relate this drawing to the work of Lowry. Coming out of School (*Tate Gallery, London*).

at colour *as* colour, for example, or shape *as* shape, purely for themselves, or engaging children in building constructions or changing the form of certain spaces. Such experiences can give the children the basis for making their own critical judgements and encourage them both to enjoy and become more aware of their surroundings and of the work of craftsmen, artists and designers.

THE USE OF A TEACHER'S KNOWLEDGE

A reliance on new techniques or easy ways of producing and presenting results in arts and crafts can lead children to be satisfied with shallow work and ultimately undermine the self-confidence they feel in expressing themselves in anything but words. We have already discussed (see Chapter 3 *The Significance of Personal Ideas*) the pressures on children to experience superficially and at second hand, whether from ready-made mechanical and imitative drawing and painting, or from the smooth and effortless tricks of television. The teacher must stand firm against this tide of mediocrity and return always to the individual child to support and strengthen his personal discovery and individual language of marks and symbols. Wherever possible he should aim to engage the child on the level of his thoughts, questions, observations and feelings, and must be aware of what can genuinely heighten perception and what are mere ephemeral gimmicks. He should also be sensitive to when a child is moved to find some personal meaning through his work, or is just lost and in need of practical help and guidance. In order to approach children's art and craft work honestly, the teacher must believe in their capacity to think, create, invent and originate. The most immediate way in which he can develop this kind of insight is through working in some creative area himself in some depth. It is through the context of his own experience that he can best understand how to use the skills and knowledge that he has, to help children. In this way the teacher's interaction with children will be dynamic and he will be able to change and adapt ideas.

PROGRESS AND ACHIEVEMENT

If a teacher believes in the value of what he is teaching and is sincere in his efforts to help children, it might be assumed that he could see progress in the work children do. However, this is not easy in an area that is concerned as much with emotions and feelings, as with mental and physical abilities. There is no body of achievement which we can say forms a common goal, and the concrete results arising from any creative work are closely related to the maturity of the child (see p. 46, pl. 25). No-one can say that a drawing by an 8 year-old is better or worse than that by a 13 year-old. The directness, spontaneity and originality of the work of a young child have a different validity from a sincere,

There is a great number of materials on the market such as 'Sticklebricks' and 'Lego' which lend themselves to all kinds of invented images (see p.46, pl. 25).

Opposite. Drawings by children of different ages:
Top. By a boy aged 4¾ – buses set out by fitting together different parts that have been remembered from observation.

Middle. By a boy aged 7 – a man with a horse, relating two objects together but still drawn as a flat pattern.

Bottom. By a boy aged 10¾ – a drawing of a landscape built up from various simple elements, viaduct, hill, house, but conceived more spatially, both in three dimensions and relative scales.

well-constructed piece by an older child. Difficult as it is to define progress in children's work in this field and to arrive at criteria by which this work can be assessed, certain guidelines must be laid down. The necessity for this is emphasized by difficulties children encounter in moving into different stages of their education. In the worst instances, where there is a lack of awareness on the teacher's part of the child's previous educational experience, a child can find this being completely discounted, only to be replaced by a different brand of the same thing; free play with materials in the primary school, basic experience with materials in the secondary school and foundation work with materials at college.

Art education is concerned with the creative growth of the child and it follows from this that progress is made when the child widens his experience. Children's work cannot therefore be usefully assessed over a short period, and progress should be looked for over a term or a year, rather than from month to month. The growth of technical skills is only one criterion. Progress also becomes apparent as the child acquires increasing sensitivity to pattern and colour, an awareness about the way in which forms and mechanisms operate, and a growing capacity to evolve images which combine personal meaning with a power to affect others.

The way in which children approach their work indicates their growing maturity as people. As one teacher put it, 'I feel they're progressing if children are willing to look for new experiences, if they seize on vital straws and opportunities, if they're willing to embark on something new even at the risk of failure.' Another teacher said, 'To me, progress is the state when teacher and children keep on questioning. When they stop doing this, it's either because the children or the teacher think they know it all, or are not involved, or have stopped thinking and trying.'

We believe that progress can be seen in these terms and that a child's work can and should be criticized and assessed, taking into account the child himself and what he is capable of. Sincerity is an essential criterion; the work should be a genuinely personal statement or experiment. The teacher should then look for the quality of the child's response to the imaginative situation or the problem, and for the degree of involvement. Thirdly, and particularly with older children, the teacher may assess the way materials and tools have been used, the approach to the problem and the kind of technical or inventive solution that has been found. Any teacher with considerable experience of looking at the work of a particular age group can recognize what is natural for the majority of children and what is exceptional. For the less experienced teacher a comparison of children's work and attempts to formulate assessments of it ought to form part of his training and be provided in every 'in service' course.

Finally, the way in which an evaluation of a child's work is expressed to him requires great care. Harsh criticism, without an attempt to find out what a child is trying to do or say, can be utterly discouraging. Its opposite, of lax approval given to every child, is meaningless. Comments should be positive and constructive, and the criteria used explicit and comprehensible, and the children themselves should be involved in finding these criteria. At the upper end of the age group, self-evaluation is becoming important and should be seen as part of a child's overall progress. If a teacher has helped children to evaluate their own work and given them sound criteria for doing so, he has achieved something of significance for them.

Examining scrap metal.

These puppets were already in the classroom when the children came in.

Display panel in a primary classroom.

Chapter 6

The Creative Climate

So far we have looked at children and at teachers, but no teaching goes on in a vacuum. It operates within a school situation, which can assist, support and help it forward, or hinder and limit it. The school in its turn is situated within a community which, too, has its own creative potential. It is important to determine the nature of the resources available within the school and in its surroundings which support creative teaching.

THE CLASSROOM OR TEACHING AREA

The first problem facing a teacher is the organization of the classroom so that it works for his or her teaching. Although specialist and non-specialist rooms will differ in many ways, each can be a meeting place for ideas.

These ideas can be initiated by the contents and layout of the room before the start of the lesson and by this means some of the assumptions with which a child comes in may be challenged. In the handicraft room of one middle school, for example, many things for children to touch and see were set out at the beginning of a series of lessons; parts of old clocks, television sets and bicycles, scraps of metal, wood and plastic, and various kinds of puppets. A boy new to the school exclaimed: 'Cor, look at those! I thought we just done wood in here.' More important, the juxtaposition of the puppets and the scrap material produced a train of ideas before the teacher so much as spoke.

Similarly, quite ordinary materials and tools displayed with care, such as paint, papers of different colours, several kinds of pens, pencils and inks, placed perhaps in front of a sheet of tinfoil crumpled to catch the light, can arouse an excited eagerness to use them.

A teacher should plan his resources to focus interest, and to stimulate questions and ideas on the topic he wants to introduce. As the children's enthusiasm gathers momentum the teacher may also want to use objects, pictures, diagrams and slides to amplify their first ideas, or to mark out points of reference which keep the work on course. This entails assembling and building up resources, in order to be able to cope with divergent interests.

95

Children in the middle years are often ardent collectors, and will help to build up collections of natural forms, fossils, stones, skeleton leaves, or of small parts of mechanical objects, or discarded kitchen gadgets. These can all be the starting point for many lines of enquiry.

3-dimensional objects require ingenuity in their display.

Children are often ardent collectors.

97

Children examining a collection of shells and stones.

Storage trays can be easily available.

RESOURCES IN THE SCHOOL

Many teachers of art and the crafts at all levels accumulated their own 'resource banks' long before any such imposing title was coined. The contents tend to be as diverse as the owners, but because they are so personally enjoyed they may be among the most useful.

This is not to decry material of many kinds currently produced commercially for school use, which can be borrowed from an L.E.A. Resource Centre or Teachers' Centre. Much material of great service in teaching will be too costly for a school to buy, and might not be used often enough to justify heavy outlay. Teachers' centres offer an increasing quantity and variety of such material, slides, tapes, film-strips, documentary discs, overhead projector transparencies, film loops, and 8mm. films. Visits to these centres to examine what is available could be very time-consuming for teachers, but in certain areas this difficulty is partly overcome by library organizers calling on the schools.

The sheer number and volume of objects a teacher may want to use, in addition to the slides, tapes and film-strips now available to him, poses a storage problem. One obvious solution used by some L.E.A.s in new primary schools is to have one wall of open shelving in each classroom unit, so that each teacher can have resource material at hand for frequent use, and to which the children also have easy access. Elsewhere and shared by the whole

Often an illustration or a passage of text produced by the teacher herself will link together material culled from other sources.

school is a larger resource centre[1] for more substantial materials and equipment. In a large school the resource centre is often under the supervision of a senior member of staff, with an assistant to organize, catalogue and issue material.

Certainly some of the most valuable resource material is that made by teachers themselves, and for this purpose certain essential facilities and equipment are needed – reprographic equipment for example.

In a smaller school, and for the teacher's own immediate use, do-it-yourself methods are necessary. Ideas for (literally) keeping tags on things may be gleaned from modern office equipment or from present day kitchens. From the first, storage boxes, files,

[1]For a full study of these Centres see Schools Council Working Paper 43, *School Resource Centres*, Norman W. Beswick (Evans/Methuen Educational 1972).

see-through plastic envelopes and coloured tags and labels simplify classification; from the second the racks and stackable shelves, plastic containers and bowls, can economize space in housing small objects and tools. The children too, should be encouraged to look round. Students in the art department of a Midlands College of Education were advised to: 'Take children into shops stocking super office equipment, fluorescent stick-ons, files, clips, etc., and let them make suggestions for equipment for their projects. Your eye for good design will help them to discriminate. Introduce them to Dymo Tape, staple guns, modern adhesives, plastic labels and folders and new methods of recapsulation with directives in clear strong colour and sensible graphics'. Resource material is only as useful as the use made of it. It goes without saying that material gathered or made by a teacher or team needs to be organized and stored so that it can be got out and put back without herculean labour.

Opposite top and bottom. Part of a large resource centre in a junior high school.

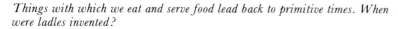

Things with which we eat and serve food lead back to primitive times. When were ladles invented?

SHARED INTERESTS

These resources of Things, visible and tactile objects, are of great value, but perhaps even more valuable are those resulting from the interchange of ideas between fellow members of staff. Although team-teaching or inter-disciplinary enquiry may not be formally undertaken in a given middle or secondary school, there is a range of specialist interests to be drawn on which can promote a vigorous two-way traffic between the visual arts and the other disciplines of the curriculum. The biologist's interest in natural form and organic pattern, the mathematician's in geometric form, the interest of the historian and the geographer in the surroundings of the school, each or all of these can feed into the teaching of art and crafts (see p. 47, pl. 29). Conversely, the art and craft teacher's knowledge of shape, colour and material, of the history of the things that man has made for his own use, and the art teacher's graphic competence, could enrich the teaching and learning of these and many other 'subject areas'.

The immediate environment of the school will often be a fertile source of ideas (see p. 47, pl. 29). The identification of fish and birds is often only a beginning.

When drawing, one sees things which would otherwise pass unnoticed.

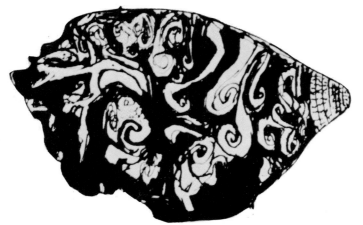

An invitation to look closely at natural form (photo Michael Moore).

Display in a book corner (photo Michael Moore).

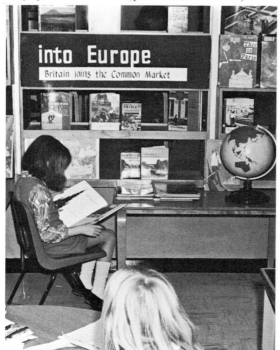

Integrated studies[1] may or may not form part of a school's policy, but the interests of other teachers can be invaluable in exploring the resources of the locality, particularly those in the natural and social sciences. In the primary school, environmental studies[2] have been undertaken for many years. Their relevance has been underlined by the growing world-wide concern for conservation, and at the INSEA Congress on Art Education and the Environment in Helsinki in 1971, biologists, town planners and architects repeatedly stressed the need to involve children in this concern, before they have become conditioned to accept the deplorable state of things as they are.

The fact that the graphic arts have a contribution to offer to these studies which can justly be called unique is less well recognized. In making the simplest of records a drawing or a diagram can state more than pages of written description, and this direct graphic statement comes naturally to children. The actual process

(Photo by Keystone Press).

[1]Integration of studies is a theme very much in the educational air at the moment, and has been the subject of a separate Schools Council project, of which the first three units have been published (from April 1972 O.U.P.) For this reason it has seemed superfluous to devote a great deal of attention to integrated studies in the present Project, other than by the accounts given in Chapter 6.

[2]Also the theme of a separate Schools Council project published by Rupert Hart-Davis. See Dialogue no 6.

of recording in visual form also sharpens observation and in itself makes for a 'visual awareness' that can be gained in no other way.

Our environment is manifestly not visual alone, but visual images are part of the warp and weft of experience. Children, like adults, may take for granted the surroundings in which they live, where they have their homes and where their parents work, never looking at them because they are so familiar. But what visual possibilities they offer! The contours of the Pennines above Huddersfield and Halifax, the great shapes of factory chimneys and the cooling towers of generating stations, the cranes and masts of shipping in a dock area, the crowded streets and neighbourhood shops in some areas of a city – any of these may offer more visual stimulus than can be fully used in the years at school.

(Photo by Keystone Press).

Artists at every level – Breughel, Rembrandt, Velasquez, Daumier, Degas and in our own day, Lowry and Herman – have shown what wealth lies in the so-called commonplace, 'the extraordinary everyday'. At the period of children's development with which we are concerned, and especially in the years from 11 to 13, children are increasingly aware of the world about them. It is therefore a period of special opportunity for helping them to become aware of its richness, and increasingly critical of squalor and visual barrenness.

To teachers who are on the lookout for them, even very small things in the most unpromising environment can provide visual stimuli. Children we observed in a Yorkshire mining village were sparked off to create a series of poems and drawings by looking closely at the frost patterns in the puddles and on the iron railings of the school playground. However such sensitivity does not come overnight. It was evident inside the school that the children had been encouraged over the years to look keenly and to enjoy the touch and sight of all kinds of objects and natural forms. Material can be brought in which will enrich the school itself, but some can only be studied at first hand, the patterns of ploughed fields or of tree-growth for example. Much of this may be ephemeral, but can be recorded in drawings or with simple cameras used by the children. A store of these records can be built up which may be invaluable as starting points for later work.

The Third-Class Carriage *by Daumier (The Metropolitan Museum of Art, The H.O. Havemeyer Collection. Bequest of Mrs H. O. Havemeyer, 1929).*

Frying Tonight *by James Fitton (Tate Gallery, London).*

Une Baignade *by Seurat. Detail. (National Gallery, London).*

In the Miners' Arms *by Josef Herman (Tate Gallery, London)*.

Children visiting a woodturning
workshop.

Apart from the physical environment there are resources to be drawn on in any community from the people who make it up: children, parents and many others. Parents' help is called on often enough, through active parent-teacher associations, for fund raising and making things for the school. It can also be invaluable in exploring local resources in excursions into town or country, to fairs, exhibitions, historic buildings and other places of interest.

A school in North London invokes parents' aid in the vacations, asking them to help their daughters explore the vast wealth of museums available. To give their exploration some direction an outline is given of the periods in the history of art and architecture that the girls will be studying in successive years in their school course.

More rarely, the talents of a local craftsman, sculptor or painter are drawn on, or perhaps of a parent involved in local industry. They may have much to offer in demonstrating or describing their speciality and the materials with which they work, some of which may be locally produced.

In some directions the knowledge of the children themselves may far exceed that of adults. In the later years of childhood many children are active explorers and may know more than some of their teachers about the workings of a grain store, silo or canal lock, where this or that plant grows, or where certain scrap material is to be had for the asking.

Preparing fibre for rope-making.

Local craftsmen will have much to offer in demonstrating and describing the processes of their specialist techniques.

Opposite centre. Tree drawings enliven a corridor. Note the corrugated card which provides the background.

Top and bottom. Materials displayed at a teachers' course.

COMMUNAL COMMUNICATION

The results of group exploration often need to be shown to other people in order to realize their full value. When, for example, a school in the Midlands organised an environmental study centred on the local canal, the headmaster took photographs of the children at work during the study. He later arranged for the parents a show of these slide transparencies together with a display of the work that resulted (see p. 47 pl. 27). A member of staff commented, 'They are really keen to see slides of their children at work'. In this way another channel of communication with the parents was opened up, leading them to further understanding of the work of the school.

The display areas in this school, as in many others, are considered vital to the school's work. They are used to capacity as a means of communication with all who pass by: the children, staff, parents and other visitors. The arrangement of displays, the lettering, and the presentation of children's work, written or visual, is critically considered. It forms part of the school's public relations. The school is aware that, apart from the direct presentation of

Children study a local canal (see p. 47, pl. 26).

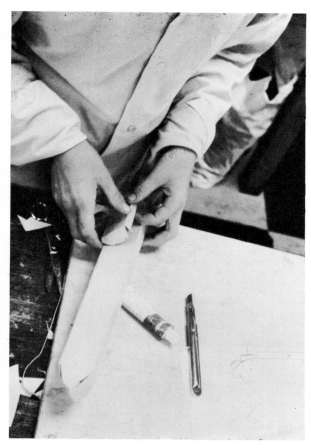

Some of the interests that developed from the canal study (see p. 47, pl. 21).

ideas, information and discoveries, *it is communicating all the time by means of its total image. What* this communicates is quite subtle. It presents the school's sense of values, its regard for friendliness, warmth, order, colour and imagination, and its respect for children and their work. The opposite image, which is regrettably still given by some schools, however unwittingly, is chilly formality, indifference, bleakness, apathy, even disorder. To spell out how one image or the other is conveyed is to risk seeming to be over-concerned with trivia, but a parallel could be drawn with the atmosphere of any home and the way it is built up by a hundred seemingly small details. In a school it would depend on the one hand on the way in which children's work is displayed, the flowers or plants in corridors or rooms, the choice of pictures, sculpture, curtains, pottery, the notices and lettering (see p. 47, pl. 30), on the other on the absence of colour, the lack of interest in children's work, the general bleakness, untidy noticeboards and litter in the grounds.

117

Display areas in a junior school. Displays of this quality affect more than those who actually produce the work.

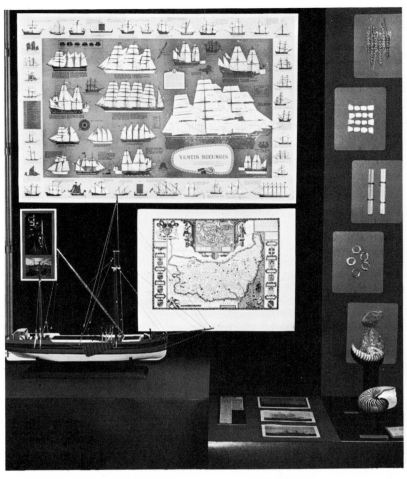

Primary school classroom.

Left. Display connected with a study of the ships that used to ply up the East Coast.

Bottom left. Part of display in primary school classroom.

Arranging an exhibition for a teachers' course (see p. 47, pl. 30).

The uncreative situation just described is fortunately less common than it used to be, but where it still happens it does nothing to stimulate the children to become visually aware or to develop the sense of responsibility for their environment which is such a crying need in the public of the future.

The responsibility for this, regrettably, can only be laid at the door of the staff who are themselves visually indifferent, probably because of the lack in their own education of any visual training. Until this is altered, it would seem that it is the job of the art and craft specialist in a school to help his colleagues to see. One member of staff should perhaps be appointed to be directly responsible for lettering, notice-boards, display and exhibitions.

Many head teachers now feel that children should encounter in school a stimulating visual environment as an essential part of their education. More than one head lays stress on the importance of helping children to notice and discuss it. A head of a middle school writes: 'The decor, furnishings and areas of display all play their part, but, more important, both young and old must be encouraged to enjoy the resulting rich environment *through observation and dialogue*'.

Just as an individual's creative work expresses his personal life, so the creative work in a school is, or can be, an expression of its corporate life. It seems self-evident that children should be involved in shaping their surroundings. They need the opportunity to personalize them, to make their mark.

Where staff are alert to them, many opportunities occur to engage children in enterprises that are concerned with the quality of social life in the school; the flowers for every day as well as for a special occasion, the meal for visitors and the table-mats and serving-dishes for their use, the printed curtains in an alcove, the group collage, or wall-painting or mosaic, or the decorations for a festival. Each may seem on its own of no great account, but the whole is greater than the sum of the parts, and can communicate a school's values more cogently than any formal speech.

It follows that there must be a concensus of opinion among the staff as to the importance of this corporate expression. No influence is as all-pervading as that of the head in such matters, but he or she needs support from the staff just as they need support from him. It is surely part of the art and craft teacher's responsibility to be articulate about visual matters, in school and out of it, and in particular to be able and ready to state verbally his beliefs about the significance of art and the crafts in children's development. It is only too easy to retire and leave the field to the Philistines, or to expect colleagues to understand without explanation.

Of all the factors within the school which make up the creative situation, we have found the most potent to be the intangible one of attitude, which is generated largely by the head of the school. From this attitude will stem the support, or lack of it, given to each subject in the practical matters of allocation of funds and space, and of shaping the timetable. Equally important is the warmth of encouragement and understanding which emanates from the head. Its opposite, a chilly indifference, can inhibit all but the most confident of teachers.

The attitude of the head affects the arts subjects perhaps more than any other, because their values are less clearly understood. The headmistress of a girls' secondary school in a London borough, whose selection of staff has helped to build up a strong art department in the school, writes: 'The presence of an art teacher on the staff of a school is symbolic. He stands as a witness to the fact that there is more to education than the transmission by teachers of a selection of explanations about the external world, and more for pupils than verbal cognitive learning . . . . . the external world exists in spite of the child, the inner world of the child exists only because he exists. The art teacher is concerned with this inner world of the child's emotions. . . .'

The headmaster of a junior high school (age group 11 to 14) in the Midlands puts a different emphasis on the contribution made by art and the crafts. Describing the present organization of the school he writes: 'The Creative Design Department contributes to the intellectual activity of the school in that the 'design' element which precedes the creation of an artifact consists of the identification of problems and the consideration of means of solving them. The second element lies in the contribution of the Design Faculty to the cultural and aesthetic life of the school, and its capacity to enrich the environment in which we live and work.'

In the passages just quoted three roles of the visual and plastic arts have been singled out, as channels of emotional expression, as contributing to intellectual activity, and as enriching the school environment. In dealing with younger children (9 to 13) the headmaster of a middle school sees these roles as fused: 'Art and craft have an important role to play in the education of the child. I cannot see where it begins and where it finishes; to me it permeates all aspects of a child's learning. I could not attempt to dictate any order of merit as the whole environment of the school is *the* centre of art and craft. Children will quite naturally choose to express themselves through the use of the media. . . . It is a legitimate way of communication, where the starting points have arisen in mathematics, science, music, drama, physical education, and an almost endless list'.

Where the Head views the subject in such a way, the contribution that art and the crafts can make to the whole life of a school is increased many times over.

SUPPORT FROM OUTSIDE

Support for a subject or group of subjects can come not only from within the school but from the attitude of the local authority, from the chief education officer and his team. In at least four county areas the importance of the arts in education has been given recognition largely because of the belief in their values shown by the eminent men at the top. This faith manifests itself not least in good practical provision throughout the area, in terms of buildings and good facilities, as well as in-service training opportunities for teachers, and appointment of specialist advisers.

Depending on whether or not there are art advisers on the staff of an L.E.A., promising ideas and developments within the school can be helped to fruition or allowed to peter out. Advisers provide a vital link between the work of individual teachers and schools and the administration. The adviser's support within a school can be of many kinds, not least in establishing good personal relationships with teachers, which are especially important when changes and uncertainty demand their co-operation. He can see at first hand a particular teacher's problems and possibilities; and on the practical side can give much help; with advice on organization of teaching-space and storage, or choice of materials and equipment. This can prevent costly mistakes. He may gain sanction and encouragement from the local authority for a promising undertaking, which an individual school or teacher would be too diffident to embark on without this support.

Outside the school his influence can be equally important, and not only through courses for teachers, valuable as these are. Where the machinery is established for consultation between the authority's administrative staff and the advisers, the latter's views can be readily available to influence educational thinking and planning when long-term decisions are being made. The adviser should be able to see the overall pattern of educational development both within his area and beyond, and be aware of the possible effect of any decisions on the future course of events. It is part of his function in the service of the schools to take the long-term view, to relate immediate objectives with long-term aims, and to keep in touch with educational developments and research at home and abroad.

Some local education authorities have a team of advisers on art and the crafts. Regrettably, a sizeable proportion still have none.

Conclusions

A PERSONAL PHILOSOPHY AS THE BASIS OF CONFIDENCE

'For me, uncertainty is an essential aspect of being alive. I am tense each time I go into a class. I believe this is valuable as it sharpens my reactions and heightens the creative response I make.'

One way of appreciating the problems that children face in their work and the significance of allowing children to find their own solutions is for the teacher himself to undertake work with new materials or explore new teaching methods. This can be disconcerting but it is only through experimentation, by doing new things, that the teacher can really develop a depth of understanding of the children, their problems and their feelings. This approach to teaching will not be a haphazard process if the teacher has a firm philosophy which provides him with his own beliefs and values.

Throughout this book we have stressed the fundamental aims of art and craft education. However, everyone is individual, and this book will be interpreted by each individual teacher in the light of his own personal philosophy and teaching experience.

Our own basis for the philosophy behind art and craft education is that we believe that it is the job of every art and craft teacher to:

- Accept the part that children's own forms and images play in helping them to relate their inner life to the outer world.
- Develop children's capacity to feel and to express feelings.
- Increase children's ability to give their ideas and thoughts visible and tangible meaning.
- Heighten children's sensitivity to visual images and forms, both in their immediate environment and in the art forms of their own and other countries.

From these basic principles we can draw certain guidelines to assist the individual teacher.

- Individual ways of working have to be recognised and accommodated; it is necessary to tolerate and encourage divergence, and to accept the uncertainty these involve.

- Techniques, skills and methods should be seen at every stage as means to an end and not ends in themselves.
- The teacher should accept a positive role, not only in providing materials, but in teaching children how they can be used.
- The teacher should be aware of the potential of the children's interests, environment and first-hand experience as rich sources of motivation and learning.
- The teacher should use the classroom as an active influence both in its appearance and arrangement.

EXTERNAL PROBLEMS

There are however, other problems which remain beyond the teacher's power to solve on his own. The increasing attention given to the special needs of children in the age group we have studied is leading to a search for a different physical and organizational framework in primary and secondary schools. This is reflected in the many attempts being made to adapt buildings, curricula and timetables for children in the upper part of junior schools and the first years of secondary schools and in the establishment of middle schools. With this has come the realization that new kinds of support are needed for teachers, both in the resources they share and in opportunities for collaboration. We would like to emphasize some of the most important kinds of support which we consider especially relevant to this transitional period of growth, when children are individually at very different stages of physical, emotional, social and intellectual development.

1. *Since time is a very important factor in the working out of personal ideas, the approach to timetabling and group sizes should allow for flexibility.*

- The practical organization for working should be adaptable at some points to enable children to work at their own speed.
- Opportunities should be made for teachers to work with small groups of children.
- For particular projects, periods of uninterrupted time should sometimes be available.

2. *Art and handicraft should be seen as inter-related activities and not in isolation.*
- In middle schools work areas for these subjects need to be adjacent, or if possible, encompassed in one multi-purpose classroom or studio.
- Teachers employed in these areas should understand and be

sympathetic to the potential of materials other than those related to their own specialism.

- Boys and girls should receive the same opportunities in their use of materials.
- The materials of art and handicraft should not be kept distinct, nor should their use be restricted or prejudiced by subject domination.

3. *Since visual and tactile learning are indispensable to children's ways of understanding the world at this age, work in art and crafts should be understood as integral to the study of other disciplines as well as being of virtue in itself.*

- Collaborative teaching on a joint venture should be possible and teachers working in teams should have the necessary time for consultation.
- Auxiliary and technical help should be seen as an essential adjunct to the teacher's work, and be used in particular to allow time for new approaches to be developed.

- In the provision of buildings:
  (i)   In middle and secondary schools, art and craft rooms should be accessible from as many subject areas as possible.
  (ii)   In primary schools, facilities for practical work should be available in each teaching unit.
  (iii) Adequate storage space, as a percentage of teaching space, should be regarded as an essential provision, or the art and craft rooms cannot function as the setting for creative work.
  (iv)   Flexibility should be considered important, so that work spaces can be adapted as differing needs arise, and so that teachers and children have the opportunity to change the environment in which they work.

THE SPECIALIST TEACHER

4. *The enthusiasm, knowledge and conviction of a specialist teacher is indispensable to the creative work and development of children in this age range, whether they be in a junior, middle or secondary school.*

- It is through his personal experience in depth that the specialist can recognise and realize the quality and potential that children's ideas can have.
- It is essential that such a specialist sees his role and context beyond the narrow confines of his own speciality.
  (i)   He needs to see and use connections not only with other

creative materials, but in other subject areas and activities in the school.

(ii)   He needs to take part in team work with other specialists and non-specialists and to work in other areas of the school curriculum than his specialist one.

(iii)   He should likewise involve other specialists and non-specialist teachers in his own special area.

(iv)   He should use his special position to initiate and advise in matters of display and visual education throughout the school.

5. *The school environment – internal and external – should be seeen as a means of enhancing children's experience and of developing their visual awareness.*

There should be a concerted policy in the school to this end. All teachers should be urged to consider themselves as responsible for the visual environment within the school, with perhaps one member of staff or the whole art and craft team taking overall responsibility.

6. *A strong advisory service, with specialist and general advisers working in a team, is essential, because*

- Through personal contact the best that is happening in education is supported and encouraged.
- Continuity and balance can be maintained in the overall development of the education service through personal visits, courses and conferences.
- Good working relationships between schools and the central administration can be established on all matters of philosophy, planning and financing.

Appendix 1

Art and the Education
of Teachers

It is not our intention to make a general survey of teacher training. Extensive literature on the subject in the form of reports, books and articles, has already been published. Our recommendations are based on observation and experience acquired not only in the course of this Project, but during years of practical work with students and with 'in-service' training. They fall under the following categories:

- Aspects common to all art and craft teachers.
- The special requirements of the middle school.
- The art college and teacher training.
- Art and the education of the graduate teacher.
- The art adviser.
- 'In-service' training.

ASPECTS COMMON TO ALL ART AND CRAFT TEACHERS

Objectives and Assessment

We suggest that art, craft and handicraft departments in colleges of education formulate more clearly their objectives in training teachers, and that they should question why they do what they do. They should consider whether the examination in art, craft and handicrafts relates sufficiently to these objectives, and analyse whether the many complaints by colleges and examiners about over-emphasis on assessment have justification. The final responsibility may lie with the examining body, but the students' views should also be ascertained as to the criteria required in the very personal task of assessment in art and craft teaching. This would encourage students to extend their thinking and to move away from the attitude of 'them' and 'us'. They are themselves about to enter positions where they will be called upon to assess children's work.

The Teacher's Personality

This redefinition of objectives should also lead to the treatment of teachers as individuals mature enough to be given a share in decision-making and to pursue any deeply held interests. Teachers exert their influence as much through their personalities as by being practitioners of skills or repositories of knowledge. Their training, therefore, should not only be concerned with their main subject but should aim to develop them as persons. If the education of the individual is divorced from that of the teacher, this can only have a negative effect on the personality of the student.

Continuity of Experience

Continuity is considered to be essential in a child's development, yet all too often is ignored in a student's training. Colleges should take into account the student's previous experience and special interests. Often it is assumed that these bear little or no relation to his work in the training department. This can cause confusion and make it more difficult for the student to adapt himself to the new demands made on him during the first years of his training.

Choice of the Main Field of Study

Students should not be compelled to choose their main subjects before they come to a college of education, at a time when they are often trapped by what was offered to them at school, and influenced by their reactions to the teachers there. This problem is resolved in many colleges by arranging the first half year so that students can see the approach and scope of the subjects that interest them, within the context of the college. There might also be more opportunities for students to have the chance in their final year of moving to another college (as suggested in the James Report) for an advanced course not offered in the 'home' college. This could be a subject course or might be a specific course in preparation for middle school training. It would also enable colleges to build up a few departments staffed by teachers of distinction working as a team over some years rather than as isolated individuals spread thinly among the colleges.

Time in Colleges of Education

A student specialising in art needs long periods of time to himself to develop his ideas. Moving arbitrarily from one experience to another can be confusing and frustrating; as one student commented, 'It fragments the personality and negates the contribution the Arts can make'. Similarly all primary school teachers should have time both to handle a range of materials and extended opportunity to work in one in depth. Certain colleges arrange for students to work for three complete weeks at one area, perhaps sculpture, music, or biology. This allows for study and involvement in depth, otherwise impossible in the normal week. Not only is more work accomplished in three consecutive weeks than 15 separate days, but experience also confirms that this type of deep involvement in a chosen activity always extends the personality and can effect lasting change.

A Common Course

We suggest that students training in specialist colleges to become teachers of art, craft and handicraft should be trained together for at least part of their course. The present system of separate specialist training for these subjects causes unnecessary friction and creates needless barriers. If however, at least one term could be spent in the other environment, e.g. A.T.D. students in the handicraft department and vice-versa, this would provide opportunities to meet, mix and learn the other's language. Where colleges provide training for art, craft and handicraft, there could be a common first term.

Collaborative Studies

There should be opportunities for all students, and particularly for middle school student teachers, to work in close contact with students from other disciplines in work groups, in discussion and in collaborative teaching projects in schools. This would bring the contribution of the art teacher into focus and also enable each teacher to justify his contribution in a wider context. By emphasizing the importance of integrated studies we are not suggesting a rejection of traditional disciplines; we wish to encourage an awareness of the relationship between them and to stress that life does not present itself to us within the boundaries of traditional school disciplines.

School Practice

We recommend that student teachers, either individually or in pairs, should initially teach small groups of schoolchildren before being confronted with the full class. This will underline the fact that education is something which happens between persons and avoids the assumption of an authoritarian attitude through fear of discipline problems.

REQUIREMENTS IN THE MIDDLE SCHOOL

Courses for Specialist and Semi-Specialist Teachers

There should be more courses of training for the semi-specialist and the specialist teacher in art and craft in the middle school. The work demands a wide knowledge and an integrated approach to learning. It includes not only the pastoral attitude of the primary school teacher but also requires a more detailed knowledge of a number of crafts, as children of 12 to 13 demand more skill and more access to technology. Another necessary quality is the ability to act as art, craft or handicraft adviser to other members of staff. We suggest that some A.T.D. courses or colleges of education should provide this kind of specific training.

ART IN THE EDUCATION OF THE GRADUATE TEACHER

Many graduate teachers, including of course those who become heads of schools, have had no experience at all of the visual arts since their early teens. A boy or girl likely to go on to a university is frequently advised to drop art at fourteen or so in order to specialize. Except in a relatively small number of universities where there are departments of fine art, university students may never encounter, mix with or enter into discussion with students of art, either in their undergraduate years or their postgraduate training.

Unless by fortunate personal circumstances, therefore, the graduate teacher may have little understanding of the values of the visual arts and little sympathy for them. Conversely, the specialist teacher of art or of handicraft, trained in a separate institution, may find little ground in common with his university-trained colleagues. In all postgraduate training there should be opportunity for students to handle and understand materials and to do creative work.

THE ART COLLEGE AND TEACHER EDUCATION

There is at present a tendency among specialist art teachers to focus on the development of their personalities as artists during their four years' training at colleges of art. If education is mentioned, it is often in a perjorative way. Yet the majority of these students will become teachers in schools or art colleges, relying on the short eight months at the end of their course for their understanding and appreciation of children and education. This does not give the students a fair chance to judge their potential as teachers, nor does it give the selectors sufficient grounds to assess them. We therefore recommend that the opportunity to gain some insight into the world of education should not only be offered, but presented fairly, to students of colleges of art. Although they are deeply involved in their own work during their last two years of college, short courses should be introduced which include talks, visits and opportunities to teach in small groups. This could be done either during the second year or during the long vacation at the end of that year, and it would provide a valuable introduction to a field in which many will later be involved. It might be made more effective if the students looked at the wider implications of art in the community, of which teaching is only one aspect.

ART ADVISERS

Only a limited number of L.E.A.s have art and craft advisers. Those that have bear striking witness to the difference this has made to teachers. The encouragement, skilled advice, the open-ended working situations either in Teachers' Centres or more specialised areas, provide teachers with a valuable opportunity to share experiences and to establish the liaison which should exist between all advisory specialists. Also, as an integral part of improved induction facilities for new teachers, the advisory staff in local authorities will need strengthening.[1]

IN-SERVICE TRAINING

We are in agreement with recommendations for 'in-service' training laid down by the James Report[2] and in the White Paper. Courses lasting one term could take place in colleges and departments of education, teachers attending one day a week, with a full week at the beginning and end of each term. Opportunities should also be preserved for some teachers to attend courses of more than three months' duration.[3] This would be considered as part of their 'in-service' training. Conversely the tutors should spend some time in the schools. We also stress the need for a greater co-operation between school and college in order to break down the divergence which so often exists between the aims and methods of each institution. Perhaps no other step could do so much to induct young teachers into their life's work without the pain and disillusion which tend to embitter their first years and distort their relationships with the children.

[1] *Education: a framework for expansion*, H.M.S.O. (Dec. 1972)
[2] *Teacher Education and Training*, H.M.S.O. (Dec. 1972)
[3] *Education: a framework for expansion*, H.M.S.O. (Dec. 1972)

Appendix 2

Discussion Material

The Discussion Material that the Project Team has produced is intended to promote discussion and questioning on the values and purposes behind art and craft education.

We believe that these Discussion Sets offer a unique opportunity for teachers to re-examine and strengthen their own approaches and beliefs about art and craft education. They will help teachers to realize some of the fundamental aspects of creative work with children, and will enable them to compare their own practice with work done elsewhere. It is important to realize that they are not presented as examples of good practice or as 'tips for teachers'.

TEACHERS' BELIEFS

It has been a constant source of surprise that so many of the teachers we have met at Teachers' Centres have been able to maintain their fundamental beliefs and enthusiasm, while continuing to cope with the day to day demands of classroom and school.

The daily routine does not often provide stimulation or encouragement and in many cases can provide active discouragement. This may take the form of inadequate facilities and finance, and an uncreative climate, as well as ancillary demands outside the scope of the teacher's training, which are costly in time and effort.

It would seem that the teachers' fundamental beliefs and values are most strongly supported by the exchange between teacher and child. The determination to allow the child to develop enables teachers to overcome the most discouraging circumstances.

USING TEACHERS' CENTRES

Teachers see Teachers' Centres, meetings and teacher training courses as opportunities to gain support and encouragement.

For many teachers the priority is to learn new skills themselves as by this they feel that they can broaden the range of knowledge at the disposal of the children. It is possible that through doing this they will come to recognize the fundamental progression and development that can occur in the teaching situation, but this is not necessarily the case.

What should Teachers' Centres offer when faced with the dilemma of introducing material and opportunities for teachers concerned with creative work? How can ideas, material and techniques be presented in such a way as to foster the growth of ideas and activities? The first concern must be to avoid the extremes of providing mere 'tips for teachers' on the one hand and vague discussion in highly specialised language on the other.

The first thing is to use the basic wish of teachers to talk and exchange ideas. They will want to talk about their common interests, their schools, the teaching situation, the children and the facilities available. They will be seeking encouragement and reassurance that the work they are involved in is valuable.

The Teachers' Centre must provide the climate and opportunity for this discussion to take place. To this end it is necessary for there to be a Group Leader who can select from available material those aspects most suitable for further discussion. He must be sensitive to ideas and directions that are discussed by groups of teachers so that ideas may evolve without over-direction, and self confidence may emerge.

It is most important that the correct climate is created so that teachers can develop their own confidence and philosophy. Communication between teachers must be direct, explicit and informative. The Teachers' Centre can provide a bank of resources and materials so that a workshop/studio atmosphere can develop which will allow for the philosophy, interests and practical needs of the teacher to be nourished at the same time.

THE PLACE FOR DISCUSSION MATERIAL IN THIS SITUATION

The Discussion Material we have produced should be seen as resource material in this situation. The main objective of this material is to direct teachers to various, often unconsidered, aspects of personal creative work with children. The sets have been used in various Centres and the attitude of many teachers has confirmed their value as starting points.

The 7 have been constructed so that they may be viewed and then seen a second time with the operator stopping slide and tape at particularly relevant points to ask such questions as, 'What would you do in this situation?' – 'Did the teacher make the best use of this opportunity?'

Experience has shown that these sets can be used effectively:

- As part of a planned programme using a number of the discussion materials available.
- Where teachers are encouraged to focus their personal experience to examine local or common problems. This has been achieved most successfully through looking at children's work that teachers bring from their classrooms.

Appendix 3

Change and the Future

Everyone who is concerned with education must be aware of the ebb and flow, action and reaction in the ideas and philosophies that are current at any one time. It may be a truism to say that innovation and change are brought about by individuals, but in our researches we have come across a number of people whose ideas seem to us to have the potential to change the way teachers feel about the process of educating.

These have been in two main areas:

groups of teachers or individual teachers who are concerned about the imbalance between the emotional and social aspects in children's learning and the intellectual and academic groups working outside the school system whose primary concern is with people and with the role of the Arts in the community.

Taking the teachers first, the most significant events have been brought about by those teachers, whatever their areas, who believe that children's ideas and feelings are of great importance and that these may be the only real starting point for their learning.

In one school a handicraft teacher stated that his aims were to create, in his room, an atmosphere of enquiry, discovery and inventiveness, where children brought their ideas, questions, knowledge and learning, to explore these through materials, in a concrete rather than abstract way. In practice, he found that he had to work against his training and to overlook many of the ideals of 'good craft practice'. There were many occasions when he felt uncertain about the direction and purpose of the work he was allowed to develop. Yet, because of the feelings of the children and their strong motivation, he gave them the time and opportunity to pursue their ideas.

This did not mean that his role as teacher became passive. He observed the way the children worked, and tried to see when and how he should intervene to help clarify or extend their ideas, give technical guidance or stimulate a new approach. One project started from a request by a group of 11 to 13 year-old boys and girls to make jewellery. The teacher found that their ideas stopped short at stereotyped conventional shapes such as the diamond, circle and triangle. In an attempt to get beyond these conventions he introduced off-cut materials in the hope that they would suggest a new line of enquiry. It did, but from an unexpected question from two boys, 'Are medals jewellery?'. From this moment the topic became one of personal adornment rather than jewellery. The teacher felt anxious about this new direction as it led the children away from recognised craft pursuits into such things as costume, make-up, masks, drama and various kinds of invention to do with decorating or camouflaging the human figure. Collectively the children handled a wide range of tools and materials and spent a lot of their free time on the project. Above all they brought their ideas forward and their questions were directed at exploring these and seeking the technical help to fulfil them.

Another teacher we met, whose subject was English, found that his approach to children ran almost totally against the rigid traditional approach of the school. He was most concerned that any relationships he made with his pupils should not follow the accepted disciplinary code but should grow from a genuine response between individuals. At the end of the summer term he offered junk sculpture as an activity, which was enthusiastically taken up by a group of 4th year boys. They eventually built a palace from junk to house their sculptures. This was erected in part of the school grounds and aroused a good deal of hostility among the staff. The boys themselves used the palace as a refuge and in this new and self-made environment they began to talk to their teacher about the problems that really concerned them. Through these conversations they became more responsible in their attitude towards authority although they still experienced considerable conflict within themselves.

Despite the strong feelings this event aroused, the teacher was given the go-ahead by the headmaster to develop another project the following year. This structure, called the Maze, became more open and allowed children of different ages to intermingle and work together. It did not shut off the group as the Junk Palace had done. The English teacher was joined by the art teacher in this project.

The following year, as the English teacher had left, the art teacher and a colleague developed a third project based on the idea of 'Metropolis'. The art teacher felt very strongly that because of the qualities which came out both in the work and in the relationships between children of different ages and the staff, these projects were both worthwhile and creatively exciting for the school community, as well as revealing and valuable to him as a teacher. He saw that quite new relationships had to be made when working with children in an environment which was totally of their creating. The normal authority role did not hold good and a far more dynamic and changing relationship had to be formed, based on mutual respect.

In all these instances, the teachers involved believed that the children's own ideas and thoughts were of central importance. They believed that they had to work outside the traditional limits of the school or subject and that to be really valid, teaching must be built on the response of those being taught. This involves uncertainty and risk, for the teachers could never be certain of the immediate outcome of their activities and as such it is a form of teaching that has to recognize risk and uncertainty.

We now come to the second area of individual influence on the ideas teachers have about education, namely individuals or groups working from outside the system. Many artists, writers and painters have become involved in direct action within their community. One example of this is the group called Visual Systems, started by two painters who had graduated from London colleges. They stated their aims as, firstly, promoting and encouraging new forms of creative activity in which members of the community, both adults and children, can be directly involved not only as participants, but as originators, and secondly, working with education authorities, colleges and schools, either through long or short term projects, to encourage the investigation of the possibilities of broadening the learning and development process. This was to be done by the extension of the classroom and general learning situation through creative and play activities in an artistic environment.

These two artists started their work on a derelict site in East London, and began to promote events and festivals aimed at involving the whole community. They invited a mime artist to join them, a troupe of actors and a group of musicians. They found that the most enthusiastic participants in their Free Form Fun Festival were children of all ages, who wanted to try everything. This confirmed their feeling that schools can be important social agents through their direct relationship to a given community.

It was through their contact with the Art Adviser for the London borough of Havering that they had the chance to work directly in a school. They erected a maze structure in the grounds of a primary school and introduced all sorts of materials and a variety of activities for both children and teachers to enjoy. Through this experimental project they learnt a good deal about schools and the problems of teaching. The vigour, originality and enthusiasm with which they worked, generated a lively response from the children. The event also brought the staff closer together than ever before to discuss, question and comment. The acting headmaster, who had become aware of the isolation in which many teachers worked, found that this outside agency made it possible for staff to move out of their rooms and begin the process of real communication between them.

The Project Officers were in close touch with all that took place, and suggested a follow-up course for the whole of the school staff. The two painters carried out this course, introducing the teachers to many processes and materials and encouraging them to use these in a number of specific ways. The teachers found the language and approach of the artists new and confusing. They wanted more direction and purpose, but the artists insisted that they should experiment rather than aim for a finished piece of work. There was a discussion which eased the difficulties, and the artists went on to demonstrate the use of some of the materials. Out of the course and the interest it engendered, the teachers were given enough confidence to want to work together at a group project back at school.

Materials were made available and the whole staff combined to develop the idea of 'Strange Planet'. Working in their rooms and then in the school hall, the project reached a climax at the end of a week with the whole school having participated. Each of the staff wrote about his feelings after the course. One wrote, 'I feel like one of those drawings you see in the Guardian, you know, when the head is cut open and hangs like a lid on a box and hundreds of people are trying to get out. Now I feel as though I have hundreds of ideas waiting to get out'. She explained that what was missing before the course was the right situation in which to talk and exchange ideas. Another teacher said that the course acted as a kind of watershed between being trained as a teacher and sharing a real feeling with others for the work they were doing. These examples describe a number of ways in which teachers have undergone some change in their philosophy and approach. This change has been more significantly concerned with what they feel about their teaching than how or what to do. To a lesser or greater degree, it has shifted their approach towards one which not only values individual response but sees this as the central point from which learning starts.

For many teachers, the importance of children being made aware of the meaning and relevance of their work has become an important issue. They see something of the need to develop children's capacity to feel and organize feeling as well as to think and organize thinking. Many teachers, by their energy, imagination and vision, are seeking ways of adjusting the balance, supported by many young people in our society who reject the facile, materialistic values that are so dominating.

How long will educational aims be biased towards the acquisition of knowledge and the capacity for thought?

Can schools in their present form, satisfactorily relate to the emotional and social development of all their pupils?

These questions must remain unanswered until the tide of educational change makes a resolution of these issues more urgent. When the time comes these teachers and artists will be seen as pioneers.

Bibliography

Art, the Crafts and their function in Education

Department of Education and Science   *Art in Schools (Education Surveys No. II)*   H.M.S.O. 1971

Field, D.   *Change in Art Education*   ROUTLEDGE & KEGAN PAUL, LONDON, 1970

Hils, K.   *Crafts for All*   ROUTLEDGE & KEGAN PAUL, LONDON, 1960

Jameson, K.   *Junior School Art*   STUDIO VISTA, LONDON, 1971

Jameson, K.   *Pre-School and Infant Art*   STUDIO VISTA, LONDON, 1968

Klee, P.   *The Thinking Eye*   LUND HUMPHRIES, LONDON, 1961

Lindstrom, M.   *Children's Art*   UNIVERSITY OF CALIFORNIA, 1957

Lowenfeld, V.   *The Nature of Creative Activity*   4TH EDITION, CROWELL COLLIER & MACMILLAN, LONDON, 1966

Mendelowitz, D.   *Children are Artists*   2ND EDITION, STANFORD UNIVERSITY PRESS, CALIFORNIA, 1963

Plaskow, D.   *Art with Children*   STUDIO VISTA, LONDON, 1968

Plaskow, D.   *Children and Creative Activity*   SOCIETY FOR EDUCATION THROUGH ART, 1964

Read, Sir H.   *The Meaning of Art*   5TH EDITION, FABER & FABER, LONDON, 1972

Richardson, M.   *Art and the Child*   UNIVERSITY OF LONDON PRESS, 1948

Robertson, S.   *Beginning at the Beginning with Clay*   SOCIETY FOR EDUCATION THROUGH ART, 1965

Robertson, S.   *Creative Crafts in Education*   ROUTLEDGE & KEGAN PAUL, LONDON, 1952

Robertson, S.   *Rosegarden and Labyrinth*   ROUTLEDGE & KEGAN PAUL, LONDON, 1963

General Education

Badock, E. H.   *Education in the Middle Years*   SCHOOLS COUNCIL WORKING PAPER NO. 42, EVANS/METHUEN EDUCATIONAL, 1972

Beswick, N. W.   *School Resource Centres*   SCHOOLS COUNCIL WORKING PAPER NO. 43, EVANS/METHUEN EDUCATIONAL, 1972

Department of Education and Science   *Middle Schools Building Bulletin No. 35*   H.M.S.O., 1966

James, C.   *Young Lives at Stake*   COLLINS, LONDON, 1968

Jones, R. M.   *Fantasy and Feeling in Education*   HARPER & ROW, NEW YORK AND UNIVERSITY OF LONDON PRESS, 1970

Leonard, G. B.   *Education and Ecstasy*   JOHN MURRAY, LONDON, 1970

Marshall, S.   *An Experiment in Education*   CAMBRIDGE UNIVERSITY PRESS, 1963

Morrison, A. and McIntyre, D.   *Teachers and Teaching*   PENGUIN, LONDON, 1969

Richards, E.   *In the Early World*   NEW ZEALAND RESEARCH COUNCIL, WELLINGTON, 1964

Smith, L. (ed.)   *Ideas Nos. 11/12*   GOLDSMITHS' COLLEGE CURRICULUM LABORATORY, LONDON, 1969

Background and Further Reading

Barkan, M., Chapman, L., and Kern, E. *Guidelines. Curriculum Development for Aesthetic Education* CEMREL, OHIO STATE UNIVERSITY, 1971

Britton, J. (ed.) *The Arts in Education* INSTITUTE OF EDUCATION, UNIVERSITY OF LONDON, 1963

Dewey, J. *Art as Experience* PUTNAM, LONDON, 1958

Eisner, E. *Readings in Art Education* BLAISDELL, MASSACHUSETTS, 1966

Fairbrother, N. *New Lives and New Landscapes* ARCHITECTURAL PRESS, LONDON, 1970

Flugel, J. C. *The Psychoanalytic Study of the Family* HOGARTH PRESS, LONDON, 1929

Gowan, J., Demos, G. and Torrance, E. P. *Creativity: its Educational Implications* WILEY, LONDON, NEW YORK, 1967

Hawkes, J. *A Land* CRESSET PRESS, LONDON, 1951

Hudson, L. *Contrary Imaginations* METHUEN, LONDON, 1966

Jung, C. G. *Analytical Psychology and Education in the Development of Personality* ROUTLEDGE & KEGAN PAUL, LONDON, 1954

Jung, C. G. *Symbols of Transformation* ROUTLEDGE & KEGAN PAUL, LONDON, 1956

Langer, S. *Reflections on Art* JOHN HOPKINS, BALTIMORE, 1958

Lansing, S. *Art, Artists and Art Education* MCGRAW-HILL, LONDON, 1969

Lowenfeld, V. and Brittain, W. L. *Creative and Mental Growth* 5TH EDITION, MACMILLAN, LONDON, 1970

Mahlmann, J. (ed.) *Art Education* (Journal of the National Art Education Assn. of America) NAT. ART EDUC. ASSN. WASHINGTON, U.S.A.

McGlasham, A. *The Savage and Beautiful Country* CHATTO & WINDUS, LONDON, 1966

Mattil, E. L. (ed.) *Seminar in Art Education* PENNSYLVANIA STATE UNIVERSITY, 1966

Mumford, L. *The Conduct of Life* LONDON UNIVERSITY PRESS, 1951

Mumford, L. *The Culture of Cities* SECKER & WARBURG, LONDON, 1938

Read, Sir H. *Education Through Art* 3RD EDITION, FABER & FABER, LONDON, 1958

Reid, L. A. *Ways of Knowledge and Experience* GEORGE ALLEN & UNWIN, LONDON, 1961

Richards, M. C. *Centering* WESLEYAN UNIVERSITY PRESS, CONNECTICUT, 1962

Robertson, S. *Craft and Contemporary Culture* HARRAP AND UNESCO, LONDON, 1961

Slivka, R., Webb, A., and Patch, M. *Crafts in the Modern World* HORIZON PRESS, NEW YORK, 1970

Smith, R. (ed.) *Aesthetics and Criticism in Art Education* RAND MCNALLY, CHICAGO, 1966

Worringer, W. *Form in Gothic* TIRANTI, LONDON, 1957

Index

Date Di